AMERICAN RELIGION

AMERICAN RELIGION

Contemporary Trends

Second Edition

MARK CHAVES

With a new preface by the author

PRINCETON UNIVERSITY PRESS

Princeton and Oxford

Published by Princeton University Press, 41 William Street, Princeton, New Jersey 08540

In the United Kingdom: Princeton University Press, 6 Oxford Street, Woodstock, Oxfordshire OX20 1TR

press.princeton.edu

ISBN 978-0-691-17756-4

Library of Congress Control Number 2017945480

British Library Cataloging-in-Publication Data is available

This book has been composed in Minion Pro and Friz Quadrata

Printed on acid-free paper. ∞

Printed in the United States of America

10 9 8 7 6 5 4 3 2 1

For Joan Chaves and in memory of Alan B. Chaves

Contents

Figures

Preface to the Second Edition

Shortly before the first edition of this book went to press in the summer of 2011, the marketing team at Princeton University Press suggested changing the title from *American Religion* to *The Decline of American Religion*. In addition to being catchier, the suggested new title seemed to accurately reflect what the book was about. The book showed that every indicator of traditional religiosity was either stable or declining, and that there was not enough new nontraditional religious practice to balance the decline. If some things are stable, others are declining, and nothing is increasing, doesn't that point to decline? If so, why not say this in the title?

In the end we decided to keep the more noncommittal title. One reason was that some of the trends I discussed in the book, such as increasing religious diversity and increasingly informal worship services, do not pertain to the question of decline. More importantly, my view at the time was that the data as a whole were inconclusive and could be read as indicating either stability or slow decline. Six years later, I no longer think the evidence is ambiguous or inconclusive. The most important difference between the original book and this revised edition—and the only important interpretive difference—is that this revised edition does not pull punches on the question of decline.

Perhaps the clearest way to illustrate this interpretive shift is to compare two sentences from the original book to their revised versions in this edition. In the next-to-last paragraph of the first chapter, the original book offered this "essential summary fact" about recent religious trends: "There is much continuity, and there is some decline, but no traditional religious belief or practice has increased in recent decades." The revised version reads as follows: "American religiosity has declined in recent decades." Similarly, here was the last sentence in the first paragraph of the original conclusion: "If there is a trend, it is toward less religion." That sentence now reads, "The trend is toward less religion."

Why have I changed my mind about this? It is not because religiosity was in fact stable at the time of this book's initial publication but started to decline since then. Nor is it because the data about American religiosity prior to 2011 are different now. I changed my mind because the decline has been so slow that only recently have we accumulated enough data over a long enough period of time to see it clearly. Some changes, such as the increasing percentage of people who say they have no religion, are quite visible with just ten years of data. But other changes are slow-moving, even glacial. Belief in God, for example, has declined since 1955 at a rate of about 1 percentage point per *decade*. Even five years ago, the available data did not provide a powerful enough lens to see the signal of general decline amid the noise of yearly fluctuations. But we have more data with each passing year, and we now have enough data over a long enough time span to discern the decline that has been there all along. The evidence of decline comes from multiple sources, shows up in several dimensions, and paints a consistent factual picture, shifting the burden of proof to those who want to claim that American religiosity is not declining. The book retains its original title, in part because it still includes material that is not about decline and in part because it is not standard publishing practice to change the title of a book when releasing a new edition. But this bolder conclusion about decline is present nonetheless throughout this revised edition.

The book has been updated and revised in other important ways. All of the figures and numbers have been updated where possible through 2014 for trends based on the General Social Survey (GSS) and through 2012 for trends based on the National Congregations Study (NCS). There are four new figures and associated discussions that present new material on declining belief in God, generational differences in religiosity, declining average congregation size, and increasing congregational acceptance of gays and lesbians. I have updated the notes to add references to relevant recent publications, and I have rewritten several paragraphs to improve accuracy and to strengthen or clarify interpretation.

All in all, I hope this updated and revised edition provides a clear, informative, and accessible account of American religious trends. That was the goal of the original book, and it remains the goal of this new edition.

Duke University
February 2017

Acknowledgments

This book began with a phone call from Peter Marsden asking me to write a religion chapter for a volume he was editing on social trends in the United States. That invitation led me to examine religious trends more systematically than I had before, and I learned that more had changed than was widely known or appreciated, and more had changed than could be described in a single chapter. A book seemed in order.

I have not produced this book alone. For the original edition Shawna Anderson, co-author of the chapter in Peter Marsden's volume, analyzed data, created tables and graphs, and helped me figure out what was changing and what was staying the same in American religion. Gary Thompson analyzed more data, created more tables and graphs, and cheerfully replicated almost every number cited in the original pages. Cyrus Schleifer made sure that figure 7.1 took account of the General Social Survey's 1984 coding change—a job that was more difficult than it sounds. For the revised edition Simon Brauer updated many of the GSS numbers, and Alison Eagle updated many of the numbers from the National Congregations Study. Alison also updated the graphs and created several new ones. This valuable help notwithstanding, I also examined all of the data myself, so any errors are my responsibility.

This book would not have been possible without two major data sources: the General Social Survey (GSS) and the National Congregations Study (NCS). Both of these data sources are publicly available, so it is easy to take them for granted. But it is appropriate for GSS users like me to acknowledge that this extraordinary resource exists in such accessible form only because of the National Science Foundation's ongoing support, the foresight of the GSS's founder, James Davis, and the stewardship of its long-time Principal Investigators, Peter Marsden, Michael Hout, and, especially, Tom Smith.

As Principal Investigator for the National Congregations Study, I am acutely aware that this resource for studying religious change exists only because of generous support from the Lilly Endowment, supplemented by support from the National Science Foundation, Kellogg Foundation, Pew Research Center's Religion and Public Life Project, Smith Richardson Foundation, Louisville Institute, Nonprofit Sector Research Fund of the Aspen Institute, Henry Luce Foundation, Center for the Study of Religion and American Culture at Indiana University-Purdue University, Indianapolis, Rand Corporation, and Church Music Institute. Many thanks to these friends of the NCS.

Elizabeth Clark, James Davis, Claude Fischer, Curtis Freeman, Hans Hillerbrand, Michael Hout, Wesley Kort, James Lewis, Peter Marsden, Ami Nagle, Melvin Peters, Robert Putnam, Tom Smith, and David Voas offered helpful comments on earlier versions of this material. Fred Appel, at Princeton University Press, encouraged me to write this book when I was still on the fence about doing it, and he pushed me to update it for this revised edition. He helped sharpen the book's original message, and he helped me think through changes to the revised edition, including further refinement of the book's central message. Jill Harris, also at Princeton University Press, managed the production process with aplomb, and Linda Truilo smoothed out remaining rough spots when copyediting the manuscript for this revised edition.

As always, my wife, Ami Nagle, has been a supportive partner every step of the way. She even pretended to take seriously my suggestion that we scotch our summer vacation so that I could finish the revisions for this edition before a September 1 deadline. She wisely let me come to the realization that this was a comically bad idea, and the resulting time on the road with our sons, Christopher and Matthew, refreshed us all. I am grateful to have a family who made pushing this manuscript's delivery date back a few weeks the best decision of the summer.

AMERICAN RELIGION

1 | Introduction

B y world standards, the United States is a highly religious country. Almost all Americans say they believe
in God, a majority say they pray every day, and a quarter say
they attend religious services every week. Some skepticism
is appropriate here. It is not always clear what people mean
when they say they believe in God or pray, and many people
believe in a God that is quite untraditional. Moreover, people do not really go to church as often as they tell pollsters
that they go. But even when we take all this into account,
Americans still are more pious than people in any Western
country, with the possible exception of Ireland.[1]

We cannot say anything definitive about very long-term
trends in U.S. religious beliefs and practices because high-

quality national surveys do not exist before the middle of the twentieth century. Still, historical studies of local communities suggest that today's relatively high levels of religiosity have characterized American society from its beginnings. Brooks Holifield, a prominent historian of American religion, put it this way: "For most of the past three hundred years, from 35 to 40 percent of the population has probably participated in congregations with some degree of regularity."[2] The weekly religious service attendance rate implied by the best national survey in 2014 is within that range: 35 percent. This overstates true weekly attendance because people say that they attend services more often than they really do, but it probably represents fairly the proportion of Americans who participate in congregations more or less regularly. The continuity is striking.

It is tempting to treat any signs of change as mere footnotes to the main story of continuing high levels of American religiosity. But American religion has changed in recent decades, and it is important to clarify what is changing and what is staying the same. As we will see, recent religious trends mainly are slow-moving—even glacial. But slow-moving does not mean unimportant, and long-term, slow social change still can be profound social change. We should not overstate change, but we also should not allow the considerable continuity in American religion to blind us to the real change that has occurred and is occurring. I will try to strike the right balance between the twin dangers of overstating and understating recent changes in American religion.

Some of the trends I highlight in this book are well known. Others are not. This book documents even the well-known trends in order to provide a stand-alone summary of important religious change in the United States.[3] I seek to summarize the key big-picture changes in American religion since 1972. I will describe rather than explain, and I will focus on aggregate national change rather than differences among subgroups. I do not try to document all the interesting differences between, say, men and women, blacks and whites, Christians and Jews, northerners and southerners, liberals and conservatives, or other subgroups of U.S. residents. I offer no overarching theory or major reinterpretation. I occasionally will comment on variations across subgroups of Americans, but only in instances where knowing about such differences is important to understanding the aggregate picture. I occasionally will mention explanations of the trends, but only when a straightforward and well-established explanation exists. This book is for those who do not know, but who want to know, in broad brush, what is changing and what is not in American religion. Those who want to dig deeper can follow the notes to additional reading. My goal is to provide key facts so those who wish to discuss, explain, or debate the state of American religion over the past few decades can do so knowledgeably.

I keep this book descriptive and aggregate because I want to keep it short. I want to keep it short because I believe this sort of factual summary should be available to the general public. Too often, we develop explanations and interpretations before we are clear about what the facts are. Too often, people interested in basic facts about American religion have to search harder than they should to find an overview they can trust. Too often, teachers who want their students to learn basic facts about American religious change cannot find a source that is inexpensive enough, and short enough, to assign in class. I wanted to keep this book short so that it can inform the maximum number of people about what's changing and what's not in American religion. For the same reason, I have erred on the side of including less rather than more methodological detail.

The trends I highlight are not the only important trends in American religion, but they are the best documented. "Best documented" is an important qualifier. I will draw primarily on the two best sources of information about these trends. One source is the General Social Survey (GSS), a survey of the American adult population that has been conducted at least every other year since 1972. The GSS, conducted by NORC at the University of Chicago, is by far the best source of available information about continuity and change in Americans' religiosity over the past four decades. Of course, no survey is perfect. The GSS's primary limitation is that, while richly informative, it has not asked people about every religious belief, attitude, or practice we might like to know about. But no other high-quality source contains as much information about American religion over as many years, and so describing the best documented trends means relying primarily on the GSS.[4]

The other primary source I will use heavily is the National Congregations Study (NCS), a national survey of local religious congregations from across the religious spectrum. The NCS surveys, which I directed, were conducted in 1998, 2006, and 2012 in collaboration with NORC at the University of Chicago. These congregation surveys do not go back in time as far as the GSS, but they offer the best information we have about congregational change since 1998.[5]

There is judgment involved in deciding what counts as stability and what counts as change. Does the four-point difference between, say, the 95 percent of people who said in 1988 that they believe in God and the 91 percent who said so in 2014 represent stability or a small decline? Does the three-point difference between the 76 percent of people who said in 1973 that they believe in life after death and the 79 percent who said so in 2014 represent stability or a small increase? "Statistical significance" is not enough of a guide, since even trivial differences can be statistically significant if the samples are large enough. Generally, I will call something a trend only if change in one direction is evident over several survey years, if several similar items trend in the same direction, or if there is corroborating evidence from other sources. Even a relatively large percentage-point difference on an isolated item measured at just two or three points in time seems too flimsy a basis for declaring a trend, and so when I have only two or three data points, the other criteria for judging something a real change—several similar items trending in the same direction and independent corroboration of the shift—take on greater weight.

This book focuses on change, but not everything is changing. In 2014, 91 percent of Americans said that they believe in God or a higher power, 68 percent said that they pray at least several times a week, 79 percent said that they believed in life after death, 42 percent reported trying to convince others to accept Jesus Christ, and 39 percent reported having had a "born again" experience. None of these numbers has changed much since the GSS first asked these questions in the 1980s. Bible reading and believing in heaven and hell also have not changed much in recent decades.[6]

These continuities, and the overall high levels of religious belief and practice in the United States, reinforce the observation that, by world standards, Americans remain remarkably religious in both belief and practice. The trends I describe in the pages that follow should be seen against the backdrop of these continuing high levels of religiosity. This stability should make us reluctant to overstate the amount of change in American religion, and it should make us skeptical when we hear that American religion is changing dramatically or suddenly. But this background continuity also makes the changes that are occurring stand out more than they otherwise might.

Time scale also is important when assessing continuity and change. Some religious beliefs and practices that look essentially stable even over a decade or two show signs of change if we take a longer view. The most important of these is general belief in God. Averaging the data between 1988 and 2014, 93 percent of people say they believe in God or a higher power. This percentage changes very little over the twenty-six years it has been measured in the GSS, which is why I mentioned it earlier as an example of continuity. But a longer view shows something different. In the 1950s, 99 percent of Americans said they believed in God, and that number has dropped, slowly but steadily, to stand at 91 percent in 2014. This is a small decline that is stretched out over six decades, and after six decades nearly everyone still says they believe in God or a higher power. The change is so slow that it is difficult to see even over a two-decade span, but combining multiple surveys over a longer period of time shows that the decline is real nonetheless. This example illustrates that my interpretive strategy and my focus on the years since 1972 make me more likely to understate than overstate change. This example also foreshadows a major summary conclusion: even in the midst of substantial continuity in American religion there are clear signs of decline.[7]

In this book I describe American religious trends under seven headings: diversity, belief, involvement, congregations, leaders, liberal Protestant decline, and polarization. Chapter 2 documents America's increasing religious diversity, including, significantly, the increasing number of people with no religious affiliation. As we will see, it is not just the country as a whole that is more religiously diverse. Our families and friendship circles also are more religiously diverse than they were several decades ago, and this probably is why increasing religious diversity has been accompanied by a cultural change in the direction of greater toleration, even appreciation, of religions other than our own.

Chapter 3 is about religious belief. Although general belief in God did not decline much over this period, closer inspection shows that fewer people express that belief with great confidence. Believing that the Bible is the literal word of God also has declined. In this chapter I also document the recent growth in what I call a diffuse spirituality, including the rising number of people who say that they are spiritual but not religious, and I show why this increase should not be understood as a counterforce to religious decline.

Chapter 4 focuses on religious involvement, which mainly means attendance at weekend worship services. It is more difficult than one might think to nail down the trend in worship attendance, not least because Americans systematically over-state how often they attend religious services. But we can see clearly enough to conclude that religious involvement has de-clined. Data that until recently reasonably could be read as indicating stability in religious involvement now unambigu-ously signal slow decline. It is not that the data have changed. It is that we have more of it, and we now have accumulated enough data over a long enough period of time to discern the signal of slow decline amid the noise of yearly fluctuations.

Because attending worship services remains the most common form of religious involvement, local congregations —churches, synagogues, mosques, and temples—remain the most central kind of religious organization in American society. In chapter 5, I document seven trends in congrega-tional life: declining size, looser connections between con-gregations and denominations, more computer technology, more informal worship, older congregants, more acceptance of gay and lesbian members—and, in some groups, of gay and lesbian leaders—and, perhaps most important, more people concentrated in very large churches. Taken together, these trends show that congregations are shaped by the same cultural, social, and economic pressures affecting American life and institutions more generally.

Chapter 6 documents several important trends concern-ing religious leaders. Religious leadership is a less attrac-tive career choice for young people than it used to be. The numbers of older clergy and of female clergy are higher than they were several decades ago. And public confidence in religious leaders has declined precipitously. Public confidence in other kinds of leaders has declined as well, but confidence in religious leaders has declined more than confidence in leaders of other institutions. All things considered, religious leaders have lost ground on several fronts in recent decades.

Liberal Protestant denominations are the only major religious group to have experienced significant, sustained decline in recent decades. Chapter 7 is about that decline. This is one of the best-known religious trends of the past several decades, but it often is misunderstood. Contrary to what many believe, this decline has not occurred because droves of people have been leaving more liberal denominations to join more conservative religious groups. Nor does the decline of liberal denominations mean that liberal religious ideas are waning. Indeed, as a set of ideas, religious liberalism steadily has gained ground in the United States, despite the fate of the denominations most closely associated with it.

Chapter 8 describes another important trend involving religion, liberalism, and conservatism. Actively religious Americans are more politically and socially conservative than less religious Americans. Regular churchgoing, moreover, now correlates even more strongly with some types of political and social conservatism than it did several decades ago. Rather than being associated with a particular type of religion, certain kinds of political and social conservatism have become more tightly linked to religiosity itself. The most and least religiously active people are further apart attitudinally than they were several decades ago, but this trend does not warrant a declaration of culture war—yet.

In this book I describe many specific trends. There are interesting details and nuances and complexities, but an essential summary fact about recent religious trends in the United States can be stated simply: *American religiosity has declined in recent decades.* Believing in life after death may have increased somewhat, but, as we will see in chapter 3, this upturn is better understood as part of the trend toward diffuse spirituality than as an increase in traditional belief. Not every trend I discuss is a matter of decline. Increasingly informal worship, for example, is a change that is neither here nor there regarding decline. And there may be specific times and places in the United States where religion looks like it is on the rise, but these should be understood as short-lived local weather patterns within a national religious climate that is in some ways holding its own but in more ways is slowly declining.

If religiosity is declining in the United States, why do people sometimes think it is holding steady or even increasing? I will answer this question in the final chapter, where I also will offer several other concluding observations about continuity and change in American religion.

2 | Diversity

The United States is more religiously diverse now than it was in 1972—a trend that began long ago. In one sense, the United States has been religiously diverse from its beginnings, when various kinds of Protestants settled different parts of the eastern seaboard and interacted regularly with American Indians, who of course had their own religious traditions. In another sense, though, the increasing religious diversity we see since 1972 continues the long-term trend away from an overwhelmingly Protestant population. This trend began in earnest with the influx of large numbers of Catholic immigrants in the nineteenth century, stalled when the United States essentially shut down immigration in 1924, and picked up again when immigration restrictions loosened in 1965.

Immigration is one important source of religious diversity, but it is not the only source. Figure 2.1 tells much of the basic story of increasing religious diversity since 1972. This figure shows how people respond when asked: "What is your religious preference? Is it Protestant, Catholic, Jewish, some other religion, or no religion?" If people say "some other religion," they are asked what religion. If respondents then mention something that reasonably can be included in one of the other categories, they are included there. For example, it is increasingly common for people to answer this question by saying initially that they have some other religious preference, and then, when asked what religion, they report "Christian." Such people are counted as Protestants in figure 2.1.

It is important to recognize that this graph shows trends in people's *self-described* religious identity. There are other ways to paint a picture of America's religious diversity, such as by tracking official membership numbers reported by churches, synagogues, mosques, and other religious communities. But religious groups define membership differently, and some groups count their people much more accurately than do others.

A person's answer to this religious preference question tells us nothing else about his or her religiosity. It does not tell us whether that person believes in God, how often he or she attends services, or how important religion is in that

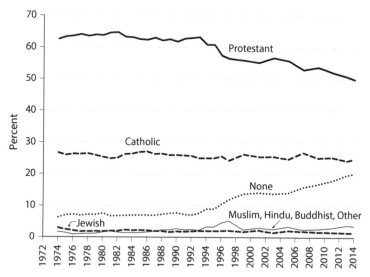

Figure 2.1. Americans' Self-Reported Religious Affiliations.
Source: General Social Survey

person's life. People's answers to this question tell us only whether they identify enough with a religion to mention that religion to a pollster, but tracking this sort of religious identification does provide a window onto religious diversity trends since 1972.

I want to highlight three features of figure 2.1. First, the most obvious trend is that the proportion of Americans who claim no religious affiliation has increased dramatically. These are the people called religious "nones," and they are the subject of perhaps the oldest joke in the sociology of religion: "There are a lot more nones than there used to be. That's N-O-N-E-S, not N-U-N-S." Remarkably, this line still elicits chuckles at gatherings of experts on American religion.

Remember, saying that you have no religion is not the same as saying that you do not believe in God or that you do not attend religious services. Indeed, in 2014, 22 percent of people who said they identify with no religion still said that they know God exists, and 7 percent said they attend religious services at least monthly. Perhaps these religiously active "nones" are among the small but growing number of people who think of themselves as "spiritual but not religious," a phenomenon I describe in chapter 3. For now, let it suffice to observe that people who say they have no religion are a lot less religious than people who claim a religious preference, but there is nevertheless more traditional religious belief and participation among religious "nones" than the zero religiosity we might expect to see.

The proportion of "nones" has been rising for a long time. In a 1957 government survey, only 3 percent of Americans said they had no religious affiliation; by 2014, 21 percent said so.[1] This increase reflects a growing willingness among the least religious people to *say* that they have no religion as well as a decline in meaningful attachments to religious traditions; but this would constitute an important cultural change even if there were no underlying changes in religious belief and behavior, and if the trend signaled nothing more than a growing willingness among the least religious to say that they have no religion. A society in which the least religious people still claim a religious identity for themselves is importantly different from a society in which the least religious people tell others, and perhaps admit to themselves, that they in fact have no religion.

Why the dramatic increase in religious "nones"? One reason is that people who are raised without religion are more likely than they used to be to stay without religion as adults. Another part of the story concerns the acceleration in this trend after 1990. After taking more than thirty years for the percentage of "nones" to rise by about five percentage points, it increased by another thirteen percentage points between 1990 and 2014, and it probably has not peaked.

The best explanation for that acceleration is that it represents a backlash to the religious right's rising visibility in the 1980s. As Claude Fischer and Michael Hout put it, "The increasing identification of churches with conservative politics led political moderates and liberals who were already weakly committed to religion to make the political statement of rejecting a religious identification."[2] The basic idea is this: If I was raised, say, Catholic or Baptist, and I am a social and political liberal who is not particularly religious, before 1990 I still would be comfortable enough with my religious background to tell a pollster that I am Catholic or Baptist. But after Jerry Falwell's and Pat Robertson's rise to prominence, heavy Catholic church involvement in anti-abortion activism, and extensive media coverage of the religious right's campaigns against feminism, evolution, and homosexuality, I am less comfortable affiliating with the religion in which I was raised. Now I am more likely to respond to a religious preference question by saying "none" because that is a way to say, "I'm not like *them*." After 1990 more people thought that saying you were religious was tantamount to saying you were a conservative Republican. So people who are not particularly religious and who are not conservative Republicans now are more likely to say that they have no religion.

I return in chapter 8 to the connection between religiosity and political conservatism. But whatever the reasons for the increasing number of "nones," this trend has created a new wrinkle in the American religious fabric. Beyond the diversity created by people of different religions, America now also has a significant minority of people with no religion at all.[3]

Figure 2.1 displays a second aspect of rising religious diversity: the increasing number of people in the United States who are Muslims, Buddhists, Hindus, and others who are neither Christian nor Jewish. From one perspective this increase is dramatic, with the number of people claiming a religious identity other than Christian or Jewish tripling from about 1 percent in the 1970s to about 3 percent today. Recent immigration drives this increase. According to the

2014 American Community Survey, approximately one in eight people in the United States is foreign born.[4] This trend continues the long-term pattern by which American religious diversity reflects American immigration history.

Recent immigration also creates a new kind of religious diversity. Immigrants to the United States before 1965 mainly were from Europe. These earlier waves of immigration increased religious diversity by bringing more Catholics and more Jews to this country. Recent immigrants, by contrast, are more likely to be from Central and South America, Asia, and Africa. Immigrants from Central and South America are overwhelmingly Christian, but immigration from Asia and Africa increases religious diversity by bringing more Muslims, Hindus, and Buddhists to the United States.

Despite increasing numbers of Muslims, Hindus, Buddhists, and others who are neither Christian nor Jewish, the percentage of these religious "others" remains surprisingly small. How can the percentage of people who are neither Christian nor Jewish still be so small, even after a huge wave of new immigrants? The answer is simple: recent immigrants are less likely to be Christian than they used to be, but the majority of recent immigrants to the United States still come from predominantly Christian countries. Even if we limit attention only to legal immigrants, two-thirds of them are Christian. Most recent immigrants are from Latin

America and are overwhelmingly Catholic. This large influx of mostly Catholic immigrants is the main reason the overall percentage of Catholics in the United States has not declined in recent decades. More broadly, the presence of many Christians among recent immigrants means that, in addition to more religious diversity, we also now have more ethnic diversity *within* American religious groups than we once had. I will return to this subject at the end of the chapter.[5]

Let me pause here to point out that commentators on American religion often overstate the number of Muslims in American society, sometimes even saying that there now are more Muslims than Jews in the United States. This is not true. The proportion of self-identified Jews in the United States has remained at about 2 percent of the total population since the 1970s, and there are about as many Jews in the United States as there are Muslims, Buddhists, and Hindus combined. Overstatements about the number of Muslims are based on inflated membership reports from surveys of mosque leaders. Still, though the percentage of non–Judeo-Christians in the United States remains small, the proportion of Americans who claim a religious affiliation that is neither Christian nor Jewish has grown and continues to grow.[6]

The third feature of figure 2.1 to highlight is the declining proportion of Protestants in the United States, another very long-term trend that has continued since 1972. In the early 1970s, 62 percent of Americans identified with a Protestant church or denomination strongly enough to mention it to a pollster; by 2014, slightly fewer than half do. For the first time in its history the United States does not have a Protestant majority. Importantly, recent Protestant decline has been concentrated almost entirely among the more liberal Protestant denominations. I describe this development in more detail in chapter 7.[7]

Religious diversity could increase in a society without having much impact on people's day-to-day lives. If different religious groups were completely concentrated in different parts of the country, or if different groups were otherwise socially isolated from each other, then the country could become more religiously diverse even though most people would still live in religiously homogeneous social circles. Different groups are indeed concentrated in different parts of the United States. There are more Catholics in the Southwest and Northeast, more Protestants in the Southeast, more Jews and Muslims in major cities, more "nones" in the West. But this spatial concentration is not severe enough to prevent extensive and meaningful interaction among people from different religious traditions.

We know this because people's families and friendship circles are more religiously diverse than they used to be. In the 1970s, 16 percent of married people had a spouse with a different religion, increasing to 24 percent in the 2010s.

Increasing religious intermarriage is especially evident if we look across generations instead of across years. Only about 10 percent of ever-married people born before 1920 married across one of the five religious categories tracked in figure 2.1; about 25 percent of those born after 1970 have married across those lines. And consider the impact that increasing religious intermarriage has on the religious diversity within *extended* families. Not only does a single interreligious marriage make one household religiously diverse, but it also makes many people's extended families more religiously diverse. Many people now have an aunt or brother-in-law or cousin whose religion is different from their own. Robert Putnam and David Campbell say that this "Aunt Susan principle" is one of the reasons why American religious pluralism has not produced more religious tension in our society. If your Aunt Susan is Catholic or Protestant or Jewish or Muslim or completely nonreligious, and you love her, it is more difficult to despise people whose religion is different than yours.[8]

Our close friends also are more likely to be of a different religion than they used to be. In 1988 and 1998, the General Social Survey (GSS) asked people to describe as many as three "good friends they feel close to," not including a spouse. The percentage of friends who share the respondent's broad religious category (the same five categories in figure 2.1) declined from 59 percent in 1988 to 54 percent in

1998. The percentage of friends who attended the same congregation as the respondent declined from 26 to 22 percent. Over a longer time span, between 1985 and 2004, the survey asked people to describe as many as five "people with whom you discussed matters important to you." The percentage of non-family confidantes in the same broad religious category as the respondent declined from 66 percent in 1985 to 60 percent in 2004. These are not huge changes, but the time span is relatively brief, and it is impressive that two different questions produce similar results. All in all, the signal from the data indicates that religious diversity has increased in many people's everyday lives as well as in the society as a whole.

A cultural trend has accompanied this demographic trend: Americans have become more accepting of religious diversity and more appreciative of religions other than their own. Increasing religious intermarriage probably is the best indicator of this increased tolerance and even appreciation, but it shows up in other ways as well. The percentage of Americans who say they would vote for a qualified Catholic, Jew, or atheist who was running for president has increased dramatically since the middle of the twentieth century, to the point where today almost all say they would vote for a Catholic or Jew, and about 60 percent say they would vote for a Muslim or an atheist. In Muncie, Indiana, the percentage of high school students who agreed with the statement,

"Christianity is the one true religion and everyone should be converted to it," dropped from 91 percent in 1924 to 41 percent in 1977. Today, three-quarters of Americans say "yes" when asked if they believe there is any religion other than their own that offers a true path to God; 67 percent say that religions other than their own can lead to eternal life. Not only is the United States more religiously diverse than it was several decades ago, but Americans also appreciate religious diversity more than they once did.[9]

Not all religions are equally appreciated, of course. American Christians are much more suspicious of Muslims than of Jews, for example, and they still are more wary of atheists than of people who believe in a God different from their own.[10] Even more troubling, there are signs that the general public's suspicion of Muslims has increased since 2001, and outbursts of anti-Muslim (and anti-Semitic) vandalism and violence can and do occur whatever the larger attitudinal trends. At the same time, however, we should not overlook the powerful dynamic that increases appreciation of other people's religion over the long term: increased religious diversity within our families and friendship circles. It seems likely that it will take several decades, maybe longer, for this dynamic to make non-Muslim Americans as tolerant and appreciative of American Muslims as they already are of persons of other religions, and dramatic events here or abroad could slow or, in the extreme, undermine this dynamic. But I expect that in the long run we will see levels of tolerance and even appreciation of American Muslims that approach the levels we currently see for persons of other religions.[11]

A final trend I want to highlight in this chapter is this: congregations have become more ethnically and racially diverse—and in a surprising way.

Sociologists and others have paid a lot of attention recently to what we might call *deeply* diverse congregations, meaning congregations that have, say, equal numbers of blacks and whites, or that have a relatively equal mix of blacks, whites, and Asians, or in which there is a sizeable proportion of Latinos among predominantly white non-Hispanics. But this sort of truly multiethnic or multicultural congregation—congregations with more than a smattering of minority presence—remains rare and difficult to sustain over the long run. And there is little increase in recent years in this sort of congregation. In 2012, only 15 percent of congregations had no one ethnic group making up at least 80 percent of the congregation. At the same time, our understandable fascination with these exciting but rare congregations has led us to overlook the real change that is happening: the predominantly white congregations of today are less predominantly white than those of 1998.

We can track this trend only since 1998, when the National Congregations Study was first conducted, but change

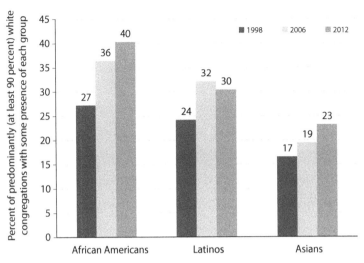

Figure 2.2. Increasing Ethnic Diversity in Predominantly White Congregations. Source: National Congregations Study

is evident even over this relatively brief time span. Figure 2.2 shows the significant increase in the proportion of predominantly white congregations that have *some* African American, Latino, or Asian members. Among congregations that are at least 90 percent white, 40 percent now have at least some African American attendees (up from 27 percent in 1998), 30 percent now have at least some Latinos (up from 24 percent), and 23 percent now have some Asians (up from 17 percent). A *majority* of those who attend predominantly white congregations now attend congregations with at least some African Americans and Hispanics in the pews. Fewer congregations, in other words, are 100 percent white and non-Hispanic. In 1998, 20 percent of church attendees were in congregations that were completely white and non-Hispanic; in 2012, only 11 percent were.[12]

Catholic churches are much more likely than Protestant churches to have some minority presence even when they are predominantly white. But the jump in minority presence has occurred in Protestant as well as in Catholic churches. As I mentioned earlier, immigration partly drives this increased ethnic diversity within congregations, but there's also more African American presence in white congregations, and so immigration is not the whole story. Increasing interracial marriage also contributes to increasing ethnic diversity within congregations. In 1980, 1.7 percent of all married couples were interracial, more than doubling to 4 percent in 2007. This rate will continue to increase since 14.6 percent of all marriages begun in 2008 were interracial or interethnic. Black-white marriages still are the least common kind of interracial marriage, but they also are increasing. In 1961, fewer than 1 of every 1000 new marriages was between a black person and white person, rising to 1 in 150 by 1980 and 1 in 60 by 2008.[13]

Interracial families still are relatively rare, but there are more now than there once were, and they have helped make American congregations somewhat more ethnically diverse. Increasing educational attainment among African Americans also contributes to this trend, because highly educated people are more likely to be attracted to the worship styles (and shorter services) more typically found in predominantly white churches.[14]

I do not want to overstate the significance of this increasing ethnic diversity in America's congregations. It is too soon to discard the old saying that 11 a.m. Sunday is the most segregated hour of the week. The vast majority of American congregations remain overwhelmingly white or black or Hispanic or Asian or whatever. Moreover, there is no increasing diversity trend within predominantly black churches. African American churches are no more likely to have some whites, Latinos, or Asians today than they had in 1998. So, besides being of limited scope, racial integration in American churches mainly is a one-way street. As in American society as a whole, increasing interracial contact within American religion mainly means more instances in which African Americans participate in small numbers in predominantly white groups. It does not mean more whites participating in predominantly black groups, nor does it mean a *large* minority presence in congregations, no matter which ethnic group is in the majority.

Our congregations, like our society, still are far from a place in which color and nationality are irrelevant, but there has been change in a positive direction. Somewhat like black-white intermarriage, which is increasing even though it remains relatively rare, increasing minority presence in predominantly white congregations represents some progress, however small, in a society in which ethnicity and, especially, race still divide us.[15]

Overall, religious diversity has increased in recent decades. People often talk about religious tolerance, but the cultural shift accompanying increased religious diversity goes beyond mere tolerance. With some qualifications, I would say that Americans now have a greater *appreciation* of religions other than their own. And just as our families and friendship circles are more religiously diverse than they once were, our religious communities also are more ethnically diverse than they were before. Increasing diversity is not just a distant fact about the society as a whole. Many people directly experience this trend in their everyday lives.[16]

3 | Belief

Some traditional religious beliefs are just as common among Americans today as they were in the 1970s. As many Americans believe in heaven and hell now as did several decades ago, and almost everyone still asserts a belief in God or a higher power. At the same time, unmistakable trends emerge in three key areas: fewer people *confidently* believe in God, fewer believe in the Bible's literal truth, and more express a diffuse sort of spirituality.

In chapter 1, I mentioned that, even though 91 percent of Americans said they believed in God in some fashion in 2014, and even though it is difficult to discern decline in this number even over a decade or two, this very large number disguises slow but steady decline over the longer term.

In the 1950s, 99 percent of Americans said they believe in God; in 1988, 95 percent said so. Another important aspect of declining belief in God becomes evident when we take a closer look at exactly what people mean when they say that they believe in God.

The General Social Survey (GSS) measures belief in God by asking people to choose from one of these six statements:

- I don't believe in God.
- I don't know whether there is a God and I don't believe there is any way to find out.
- I don't believe in a personal God, but I do believe in a Higher Power of some kind.
- I find myself believing in God some of the time, but not at others.
- While I have doubts, I feel that I do believe in God.
- I know God really exists and I have no doubts about it.

The last four responses indicate some manner of believing in God or a higher power. Those are the answers that add up to 91 percent of Americans in 2014. But when we look only at people who indicated a confident belief in God by choosing the sixth response—"I know God really exists and I have no doubts about it"—clear decline is evident in both the near and the long term.

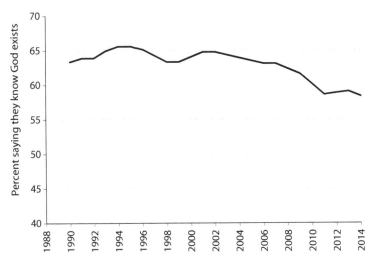

Figure 3.1. Declining Confident Belief in God. Source: General Social Survey

Figure 3.1 tells the story. The GSS first asked this question in 1988. The percent saying that they know God exists and have no doubts held steady at about 65 percent from then until 2000, after which it declines. In 2014, 58 percent of Americans chose this most confident way of expressing belief in God. Again the decline is slow, but it is unmistakable. And it is even more evident over a longer time frame. In a 1964 survey that offered this same set of responses, 77 percent of Americans said that they know God exists and have no doubts.[1] The bottom line is that both hesitant and confident belief in God have declined in recent decades, but a confident belief in God has declined faster, especially in recent years.

Belief in a literal Bible also has declined. Figure 3.2 shows the trend. This figure displays results from two different ongoing national surveys, the GSS and Gallup polls. In both surveys people are asked the exact same question: "Which of these statements comes closest to describing your feelings about the Bible?" The options are the following:

- The Bible is the actual word of God and is to be taken literally, word for word.
- The Bible is the inspired word of God, but not everything in it should be taken literally, word for word.
- The Bible is an ancient book of fables, legends, history, and moral precepts recorded by men.

Figure 3.2 graphs the percent choosing the first option: the Bible should be taken literally. Clearly, a gradual but steady decline in belief in an inerrant Bible has occurred. Since the 1970s the percentage of people who say they believe that the Bible should be taken literally declined from approximately 40 to approximately 30 percent. This is one of very few religious subjects on which two different surveys ask the exact same question over a long period of time, and the two surveys produce remarkably similar results.

Figure 3.2. Declining Belief in a Literal Bible. Source: General Social Survey and Gallup Polls

Generational turnover is an important part of this trend, with more recently born individuals much less likely to believe in an inerrant Bible than those born longer ago. Almost half of Americans born before 1910 believed that the Bible is the literal word of God, while fewer than one-third of those born after 1940 believe that. The overall percentage declined slowly but surely as younger generations replaced older generations who had stricter views about the Bible. Social change occurring in this way can be gradual, but still profound.

Interestingly, belief in inerrancy may have bottomed out. Most of the decline in this belief occurred before 1990, with the trend leveling off or, perhaps, declining more slowly, between 1990 and the present. Moreover, although people born in the 1940s are much less likely to believe in an inerrant Bible than people born in the 1910s, those born in the 1980s are only slightly less likely to believe in an inerrant Bible than people born in the 1940s: 28 percent versus 31 percent. The generation gap all but disappeared beginning with those born in the 1940s.

This leveling off probably has occurred because, of all the religious beliefs, attitudes, and practices described in this book, belief in an inerrant Bible is the most strongly connected to a person's level of education. Highly educated people are much less likely than less well-educated people to say the Bible should be taken literally. In 2014 fewer than half as many college graduates as nongraduates said the Bible should be taken literally—18 percent compared to 40 percent.[2] This difference is important to understanding the trend, because the expansion of higher education was a major social trend during the last century, and declining belief in inerrancy occurred partly because better educated generations replaced less educated generations. And rates of belief in inerrancy stopped declining in part because college graduation rates stopped increasing rapidly. Only 8 percent of people born in the first decade of the twentieth century received a bachelor's degree. That increased to 27 percent for people born in the 1940s, but the percentage of college graduates has increased only a little bit more since then—to 30 percent for people born after 1970. Higher education still pulls people away from a literal reading of the Bible, but when higher education's expansion slowed, it stopped driving down the overall level of belief in inerrancy.

Increasing educational attainment is not the whole story behind this trend. Indeed, even though college graduates are much less likely than others to take the Bible literally, belief in inerrancy also has declined among those with less education. Looking only at people without a bachelor's degree, 36 percent of those born after 1970 endorsed inerrancy, compared to 49 percent of those born before 1921.[3]

What does it mean that confident belief in God and belief in a literal Bible have declined even though some other religious beliefs have not? Part of the answer lies in the declining proportion of Protestants in the United States, described in chapter 2. Since believing in the Bible's literal truth is most common among Protestants, a smaller Protestant population will mean fewer people who believe that the Bible should be taken literally. But this is not the whole story. I am inclined to connect these developments to the attitude trends I also described in chapter 2. Not only are Christians in the United States less likely now to say that their religion provides the only path to truth or salvation, but people in general also are more appreciative of religions other than their own, and they are less tolerant of intense religiosity of any sort. Putting all this together, we might say that, even in the midst of high levels of religious belief and practice in American society, there is declining confidence in the special status of one's own religion. Believing in God, but with more doubt or hesitation or vagueness, and no longer seeing the Bible as literally true, are part of a more general shift away from seeing any one religion, even one's own, as uniquely true.

Confidence in the special status of one's own religion is not the only aspect of American religion that is declining. Indeed, this book will make clear that every indicator of traditional religiosity is either stable or declining. With one exception, nothing is going up. When it comes to Americans' religiosity, the only thing that may be increasing slightly is what we might call diffuse spirituality.

One sign of this diffuse spirituality is the small but noticeable increase in the percentage of people who say they believe in life after death, from about 75 percent in the 1970s to about 80 percent in 2014. I interpret this as an increase in diffuse spirituality rather than in traditional religious belief because belief in the afterlife has increased only among the least religious Americans and among subgroups who have not traditionally emphasized an afterlife. Figure 3.3 shows the trend in this belief separately for people who say they attend religious services at least weekly and those who say they attend less frequently than that. The pattern is clear.

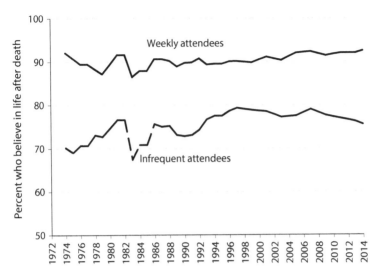

Figure 3.3. Belief in the Afterlife Increasing Only among Less Regular Attendees. Source: General Social Survey

There has been no increase in belief in life after death among regular attendees. Among that group, the level of belief was very high in the 1970s, and it is still high now. Among less regular attendees, however, believing in life after death has increased from 71 percent in the 1970s to almost 80 percent in the first decade of the twenty-first century. Belief in life after death also has increased substantially among religious "nones," from 50 percent in the 1970s to nearly 60 percent in the twenty-first century. Remarkably, the number of Jews who say they believe in life after death increased from 20 percent to nearly 60 percent in that same time period.[4]

Perhaps the clearest sign of a growing diffuse spirituality in the United States is the small but noticeable rise in the percentage of people who say they are "spiritual but not religious." This phenomenon is often commented upon, but it should not be exaggerated. The best way to track this trend is by giving people a chance to say that they are *both* spiritual and religious. The General Social Survey does this by asking two questions. First: "To what extent do you consider yourself a *religious* person? Are you very religious, moderately religious, slightly religious, not religious at all?" Second: "To what extent do you consider yourself a spiritual person? Are you very spiritual. . . ."

The vast majority of people—approximately 80 percent —describe themselves as *both* spiritual and religious. Still, a small but growing minority of Americans describe themselves as spiritual but not religious, as figure 3.4 shows. In 1998, 9 percent of Americans described themselves as at least moderately spiritual but not more than slightly religious. That number rose to 16 percent in the 2010s.

The increase in being "spiritual but not religious" is happening both because people are less likely to say they are religious and because a larger share of nonreligious people say they are spiritual. In 2014 only 54 percent of Americans said that they were at least moderately religious, declining from 62 percent in 1998. At the same time, more of that growing pool of nonreligious people now say they are at

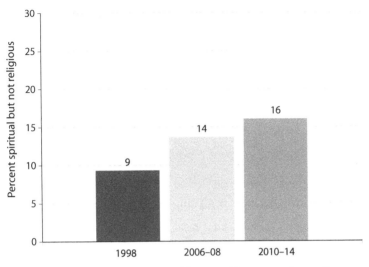

Figure 3.4. Growing Minority of "Spiritual but Not Religious."
Source: General Social Survey

least moderately spiritual: 37 percent in 2014, up from 24 percent in 1998. Nonreligious people are much less spiritual than religious people, 88 percent of whom said they were at least moderately spiritual in 2014. But, similar to the pattern we saw in belief in life after death, increased interest in "spirituality" is concentrated among the less religious.[5]

It is difficult to know what people mean when they say they are spiritual but not religious. The most obvious interpretation is that such people consider themselves to be generally concerned with spiritual matters (whatever *that* means) but are not interested in organized religion. If this interpretation is correct, then this growing segment of the population is unlikely to reenergize existing religious institutions. Nor will it provide a solid foundation for new kinds of religious institutions or new religious movements. The spiritual but not religious should not be seen as yearning people ready to be won over by a new type of religion specifically targeted to them. They may provide a market for certain kinds of religious products, such as self-help books with spiritual themes, but they probably will not create a stable, socially and politically significant organizational expression. The spiritual-but-not-religious phenomenon is too vague, unfocused, and anti-institutional for that. It is best seen as one aspect of Americans' overall softening involvement in traditional religion (the subject of the next chapter), and as part and parcel of a growing skepticism in American society about the value of organizations and institutions in many spheres of life, including religion.[6]

4 | Involvement

There is more to religious involvement than participation in organized religion, and some research and writing about American religion creates the impression that new and unconventional forms of religiosity are swamping more traditional practice. However, religious involvement in the United States still mainly means attending weekend worship services. Only 1 percent of people who say they attended some kind of religious service in the past week went only to something other than a conventional weekly worship service. More people say that they pray than attend services, but when Americans practice religion with others outside their own home it almost always means they attend a religious service at a local church, synagogue, mosque, or temple. So tracking trends in religious involvement is primarily a matter of tracking trends in religious service attendance. As we will see, attendance trends are more difficult to interpret than one might expect, and, until recently, reasonable people might have disagreed about whether the main story is one of stability or decline. It is now clear, however, that Americans' religious involvement has indeed declined in recent decades.

Tracking attendance trends is easier said than done because people do not always tell the literal truth when they answer survey questions about their behavior. We know from comparing survey responses to the number of empty bottles and cans in people's trash that people drink more alcohol than they say they do. We know from comparing survey responses to voting records that many people say that they voted in the most recent election even when they did not. Similarly, people say that they go to church more often than they really do. We know this because, when we compare how many people say they attend services with how many people actually appear at services, we find that many more people say they attended than actually did. The exaggeration also becomes clear when we compare results from two different types of surveys.

One type of survey, the most common kind, asks people directly about their attendance. The Gallup Organization, for example, asks people, "Did you, yourself, happen to attend church or synagogue in the last seven days?" The General Social Survey (GSS) asks people, "How often do you attend religious services?" Answers to this question are placed into categories ranging from "never" to "several times a week."

Another kind of survey assesses how often people attend religious services without asking them about it directly. In these surveys, called "time use" or "time diary" studies, people are asked to describe what they did, hour by hour, the day before they are being interviewed. Researchers can then see whether people interviewed on a Monday, for example, mentioned attending religious services the day before. Remarkably, these time diary studies find much lower religious service attendance rates than conventional surveys find. Indeed, they find attendance rates that are much closer to what we find when we count heads at services. In the 2014 American Time Use Survey, for example, 21 percent of people reported attending religious services. By contrast, the weekly attendance rate implied by the 2014 GSS, using the direct approach, was 35 percent.[1]

I do not think people exaggerate their religious service attendance because they want to appear pious or virtuous to the interviewer. Rather, I think the exaggeration arises mainly because people want to tell interviewers truthfully that they consider themselves to be religiously involved. Even when a survey question asks literally and narrowly about attendance, people may interpret it as asking whether they generally are affiliated with a place of worship. In this scenario, people exaggerate their literal attendance because they are trying to report accurately their identities as religiously active people who attend services regularly, if not weekly. From this perspective, the standard survey questions that directly ask about attendance pick up the percentage of people who think of themselves as attached to a place of worship even if they attend less than weekly. And, of course, more Americans are connected at some level to congregations than attend on any given week. The indirect approach of the time diary produces a lower, more accurate weekly attendance rate because it does not lead people to exaggerate in order to communicate that they are religiously involved. Another fact bolsters this interpretation: those who exaggerate are regular attendees of religious services—just not as regular as they say they are.[2]

No "fact" about American religion is more widely repeated than the claim—based on surveys that ask people directly about their attendance—that 40 percent of Americans attend religious services in any given week. But this oft-repeated claim is false. The true attendance rate is closer to 20 percent than to 40 percent. By world standards this still is a high participation rate, but it is not as high as commonly believed.

Fortunately, even though standard surveys produce inflated attendance rates, we still can use them to track change

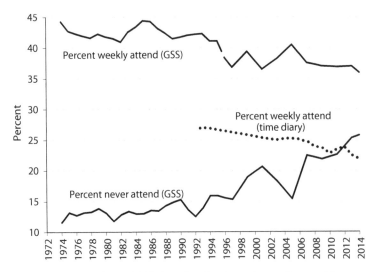

Figure 4.1. Declining Religious Service Attendance. Source: General Social Survey and American Time Use Survey

because the gap between reported and actual attendance appears to have remained approximately the same in recent decades. Figure 4.1 shows attendance trends using both the GSS and time diaries. And it shows trends both for weekly attendance and for the percent who never attend.[3]

Note first that the weekly attendance rate implied by the GSS is much higher than that calculated from time diaries. Throughout the years covered by both surveys, the weekly attendance rate implied by the GSS is about 15 percentage points higher than the rate produced by the time diaries. The time diary numbers give the percentage of respondents who, when asked to describe what they did on a Sunday, reported attending religious services. People attend services on days other than Sundays, but the vast majority of people who attend services on days other than Sunday also attend on Sunday. Jews and Muslims, of course, traditionally hold services on days other than Sunday, but there are not enough service-attending Jews and Muslims to much affect these numbers. Taking account of all those who attend religious services only on days other than Sunday would raise the weekly attendance rate calculated from time use studies by only two percentage points. All in all, the lower numbers produced by the time diaries are more accurate than the higher numbers produced by direct questions.

What about the trend? In a word, religious service attendance has declined. This trend, and changes over time in how observers have interpreted it, nicely illustrates the power of having more data over a longer time span. If we were looking at this trend as recently as 1994, we would have concluded that there is little sign of decline. And even if we were looking at it as recently as 2008, we might have concluded, as I did in this book's first edition, that, although there were hints of decline, reasonable people could disagree about whether the big picture was one of slow decline or stability. Now, however, it is clear that the story is slow decline since the mid-1980s. Religious service attendance was essentially stable, and maybe even increased slightly, from the 1970s to the 1980s, but it has declined since then.

The rate of decline has been slow—about one-quarter of a percentage point per year since 1984—but real. The decline has been slow enough that it was difficult to discern even with thirty years of data. Only with the more powerful lens provided by more than forty years of data have we been able to see through the noise of yearly fluctuations to discern that attendance in fact has been slowly declining for decades. Decline also is evident in the time diary reports. Moreover, since the U.S. population currently is growing by about 0.7 percent each year, an annual decline in the attendance rate of about one-quarter of a percentage point means that the absolute number of regular attendees, not just the percentage, also is declining.[4]

At the same time, the percent of people who *never* attend religious services, while still relatively small, has doubled, going from 13 percent in 1990 to 26 percent in 2014. How can the weekly attendance rate be declining so slowly when so many more people never attend at all? This is happening because the increasing number of people who never attend mainly comes from people shifting from very infrequent attendance to nonattendance. This shift has little effect on the weekly attendance rate, since people who attend a handful of times a year provide only a negligible bump to the overall percentage of people who attend in any given week. Much like the rising percentage of religious "nones" documented in chapter 2, the rising percentage of people who never attend services mainly represents a change from a culture in which quite unreligious people still cling to their religious identities, if only with their fingernails, to one in which these people completely let go of those identities.

Taking a longer view, other evidence shows that the decline in religious service attendance began at least fifteen or twenty years before the mid-1980s, especially for Catholics. Time diaries also register a decline in that earlier period, from approximately 40 percent in 1965 to about 27 percent in 1993. Overall, then, the basic story about religious service attendance is that, with the exception of a brief period of stability, or possibly slight increase, from the mid-1970s to the mid-1980s, it has been slowly declining for sixty years.[5]

Children's religious participation provides another window onto religious involvement trends. Religious involvement in youth is one of the best predictors of religious involvement in adulthood, and so trends in the extent to which people grow up in religiously active households foreshadow future trends in involvement. Figure 4.2 focuses on religious socialization trends by tracking the percentage of people raised by religiously active parents. The average American lives a long time, and whether or not our parents were religiously involved when we were, say, sixteen years old does not change as we get older. This means that the percentage of Americans raised in religiously active households will change slowly even if generational differences in

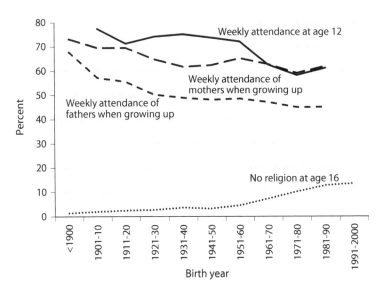

Figure 4.2. Declining Religious Socialization. Source: General Social Survey

the prevalence of childhood religious socialization are substantial. Limiting attention to year-by-year change would lead us to overlook the long-term generational change that is afoot. That is why figure 4.2 shows the trends across generations rather than across years.[6]

Generational differences in childhood religious socialization are appreciable. More recently born individuals are more likely to be raised in nonreligious households. The pace of change increases beginning with people born after 1940. Childhood weekly attendance declines from nearly 80 percent among people born before 1910 to approximately 60 percent for those born after 1970. About 70 percent of respondents born in the first part of the twentieth century report that, while they were growing up, their mothers were weekly attendees, a figure that declines to about 60 percent for people born in the latter part of the century. Most striking of all is a steady decline in the percentage of people who report growing up with religiously active fathers—from nearly 70 percent for those born before 1900 to about 45 percent for those born after 1970. There can be little doubt that, as the twentieth century unfolded, fewer American children grew up in religiously active households. This conclusion is reinforced by studies that track attendance trends among children and those that compare attendance rates among young people at different points in time.[7]

The long-term consequences of these generational differences in religious socialization are evident in figure 4.3. This figure tracks monthly (or more often) religious service attendance rates for nine birth cohorts as they age. The slight increase in attendance in the 1980s that we saw in figure 4.1 is evident here as slightly increasing attendance within each cohort from the mid-1970s to the mid-1980s. But the most striking feature of this figure is that each successive cohort attends at a slightly lower rate than the cohort before it. Those born between 1965 and 1974 attend slightly less than those born between 1955 and 1964, who attend slightly less than those born between 1945 and 1954. Some of the cohort differences are larger than others, and

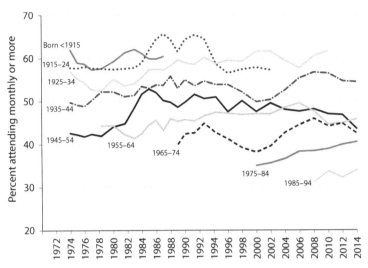

Figure 4.3. Cohort Differences in Religious Service Attendance.
Source: General Social Survey

there are some complexities in the picture, but the general pattern is clear. Moreover, virtually all of the decline in attendance since the mid-1980s has been produced by these generational differences. Attendance has declined because older, more religious, cohorts inexorably leave the scene, to be replaced by younger, less religious cohorts.[8]

The same is true for other aspects of religiosity. Graphs analogous to figure 4.3 but focused on the proportion of Americans who say they have a strong religious affiliation or who say that they know God exists look basically the same. For these aspects of religiosity as well as for attendance, decline is driven by generational replacement. This is also true, not incidentally, of religious decline throughout Europe, and in Canada and Australia as well. Social change that is driven in this way by cohort replacement has the interesting feature that it can occur even if few individuals become less religious over their lifetimes. If we are slightly less religious than our parents, and if our children are slightly less religious than us, the long-term consequence is religious decline.

To summarize, Americans' religious involvement has declined over recent decades. Aggregate weekly attendance at worship services has declined, and the percent of people who never attend has steadily increased. Each new cohort of individuals attends religious services less than did earlier cohorts at the same age, and each new generation of Americans is less likely to be raised in a religiously active family than were earlier generations. Moreover, more extensive forms of involvement also have declined. The GSS occasionally asks people how often they participate in a religious congregation's activities beyond attending services. Seventeen percent of Americans in the 1990s said they did this nearly every week or more, declining to 11 percent in the 2010s. The trend is the same for people who are regular attendees.

Religious involvement has declined in part because American family and household structures have changed. The primary social base for conventional, mainstream American religion remains the traditional family: people living in two-parent-plus-children households, along with older people who lived in such households until their grown children left home. Combining all the General Social Surveys from 1972 to 2014, married people with children at home are much more likely than divorced, separated, or never married people with no children to say that they attend services at least weekly: 32 percent compared to 19 percent. Childless married couples attend at a rate in between that of the non-married and the married with children: 24 percent of these people say they attend weekly.

The strong connection between family structure and religious involvement is important because the proportion of Americans living in traditional families, meaning two-parents-plus-children, has dramatically declined in recent decades. Compared to several decades ago, people now marry and have children later, more people do not marry at all, more people remain childless, and more people with children are single parents. These are big changes. Just looking at people age twenty-five and older, the proportion who never married more than doubled from 9 percent in the early 1970s to 20 percent in 2012. Childlessness among women in their forties doubled from about 10 percent of women in the 1970s to about 20 percent in the first decade of the twenty-first century, although it since has declined to about 15 percent.

Add divorce and rising numbers of single-parent households to this mix, and the result is a dramatic decline in the traditional families that have been the lifeblood of American religion. In the 1970s, 56 percent of American adults between twenty-five and sixty years old were married with kids at home. In the 2010s, 26 percent live in that situation. These family changes also help to explain why each generation is somewhat less religious than the previous one.[9]

Religious involvement is declining because one of the most religiously involved demographic groups—married couples with children—is shrinking as a proportion of American society. Another demographic trend—more elderly people—may be a countervailing force, since older people are among the most religiously involved segments of American society, but one of the reasons older people are more religious is because more of them lived in traditional families when they were younger. As younger cohorts inexorably replace older cohorts, the elderly population will include more and more people who did not spend their adult years in traditional families and who did not attend religious services regularly. So the aging of the American population will help mitigate religious involvement decline for a while longer, but not forever.

The strong connection between religious involvement and family life in the United States points to a larger conclusion. Religious involvement trends are not fundamentally altered by specific events such as terrorist attacks or natural disasters or financial crises. Such events may cause some changes in religious involvement, but those changes usually are short-lived. They are blips in the longer-term trends; they are today's weather, not the climate. More fundamental and lasting change in American religious involvement is produced by demographic changes, especially changes in family and household patterns. These demographic trends are where we should look for clues about the future of American religious involvement.

5 | Congregations

There are more than 300,000 religious congregations—churches, synagogues, mosques, and temples—in the United States. More than 60 percent of American adults have attended a service at a religious congregation within the past year, and about one-quarter attend services in any given week. There is more to religious involvement than participation in organized religion, but when Americans practice religion with others outside their own home, it almost always means they attend a religious service at a local church, synagogue, mosque, or temple. Congregations remain the most significant social form of American religion.[1]

In this chapter I document seven trends in congregational life: declining size, looser connections between congregations and denominations, more computer technology, more informal worship, older congregants, more acceptance of gay and lesbian members and, in some groups, leaders, and, what is perhaps most important, more people concentrated in very large churches. (An eighth significant congregational trend—increasing ethnic diversity within predominantly white congregations—was described in chapter 2.) Taken together, these trends show that congregations are shaped by the same cultural, social, and economic pressures affecting American life and institutions more generally.

The National Congregations Study (NCS), which began in 1998, is the primary source of information for most of the trends I describe in this chapter.[2] As in the chapters on American religion as a whole, I will focus on change, but here again not everything is changing, and some of the continuity may be surprising. Even though both major political parties continue their efforts to mobilize churches, for example, congregations in 2012 reported about the same levels of political involvement that they reported in 1998. And even though there are many more female clergy today than there were several decades ago—as well as more cultural acceptance of female clergy and large increases in the number of congregations led by women within some religious groups—on a national level there has been no increase in the percentage of congregations led by women. It was 11 percent in 1998, and it was still 11 percent in 2012.[3]

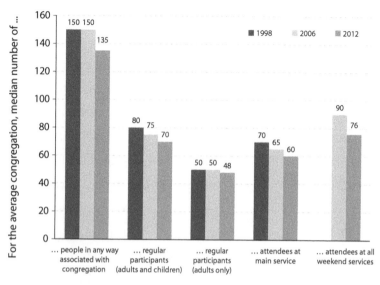

Figure 5.1. Decreasing Average Size of Congregations. Source: National Congregations Study

But a lot has changed, even since 1998. For starters, the declining religious involvement I documented in chapter 4 manifests itself as well in the declining size of the average congregation. Figure 5.1 shows the trend in median congregational size for five different size indicators: the total number of people associated with the congregation's religious life; the number of people, including adults and children, who regularly participate in the congregation's religious life; the number of adults who regularly participate; the number of people who attended the previous week's main worship service; and the total number of people who attended all weekend worship services over the past weekend. (This last question was not asked in 1998.)

The picture is clear: average congregational size declined between 1998 and 2012. The median number of people involved in the congregation in any way dropped from 150 in 1998 and 2006 to 135 in 2012; the median number of regular participants declined from 80 in 1998 to 75 in 2006, and to 70 in 2012; the median attendance at the main worship service was 70 in 1998, 65 in 2006, and only 60 in 2012; and median attendance at all weekend worship services declined from 90 in 2006 to 76 in 2012. These are not large declines, but there is a consistent signal.[4]

It is worth noting that, after two NCS waves, average congregational size appeared not to have changed between 1998 and 2006. This is another example of how more data over a longer time span is analogous to building a more powerful telescope. It sharpens our vision. We can now see that average congregation size did indeed get smaller between 1998 and 2006, but the decline was slow enough that we could not discern the signal from the noise before the addition of the 2012 data.

A second important congregational trend is that organizational ties between congregations and national denominations have loosened. The clearest indication of this trend is the growing proportion of congregations that are unaffiliated with a denomination. This does not apply to

Roman Catholicism. There is no such thing as an unaffiliated Roman Catholic parish, and Catholic parishes remain as tightly bound as ever to their dioceses and bishops, at least when it comes to official organizational structure. The NCS does not contain enough synagogues and other non-Christian congregations to meaningfully assess these congregations' connections to larger religious institutions, and so here I am talking just about Protestant churches, where the trend is clearest.

About one in four Protestant churches is now independent of any denomination, and about one in five Protestants now attends those independent churches. As figure 5.2 displays, the number of Protestants attending independent congregations increased from 14 percent in 1998 to 21 percent in 2012. If the unaffiliated congregations were all in one denomination, they would constitute the second-largest in number of participants (behind only the Roman Catholic Church) and the largest in number of congregations. Although most Protestant congregations are denominational, a noticeable and growing minority are not formally affiliated with any denomination.

An increase of seven percentage points in the number of people attending independent Protestant churches may not seem like much, but keep in mind that this has occurred just between 1998 and 2012. Moreover, these numbers probably understate the cultural significance of this trend,

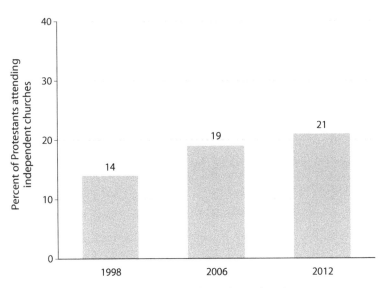

Figure 5.2. More Protestants in Independent Churches. Source: National Congregations Study

since denominational affiliations seem to be decreasingly important to congregations and their members even when they exist. Nearly two-thirds of Protestant megachurches formally belong to a denomination, for example, but many hide or downplay those connections. And NCS data show that, even though the annual income of denominationally affiliated Protestant churches increased faster than inflation between 1998 and 2012, the amount of money these congregations passed on to their denominational offices declined in real terms over these years. The minority of congregations who gave nothing to their denominations increased slightly from 11 percent in 1998 to 16 percent in 2012. And those who gave something gave a smaller proportion of their income in 2012 than they did in 1998: 7 percent compared with 10 percent. Some congregations reduced contributions to their denominations to protest denominational policies or priorities, but the weakening financial contributions of congregations to their denominations is a longer-term trend driven mainly by the rising costs of running a local congregation.[5]

A third congregational trend evident since 1998 is dramatically greater use of computer technology. Figure 5.3 shows the key numbers. The number of congregations with websites increased from 17 percent in 1998 to 56 percent in 2012. The number using visual projection equipment in their main worship service increased from 12 to 35 percent during the same time period. And the number using email to communicate with members increased from 21 to 59 percent between 1998 and 2006. The survey did not ask about email use in 2012 but did ask about Facebook pages: 40 percent of congregations had a Facebook page in 2012. These are very large increases. They imply, for example, that each year since 1998 another 10,000 congregations created a website. Eighty-three percent of religious service attendees are now in congregations with websites, and 45 percent are in congregations using visual projection equipment in the main worship service. In 2006, 79 percent of people who attended religious services were in congregations that

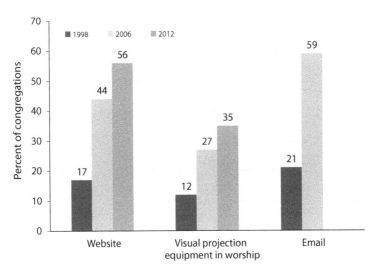

Figure 5.3. Increasing Use of Computer Technology. Source: National Congregations Study

communicate with members via email. That number surely is even higher today.

Congregations across the social and religious spectrum are increasingly embracing these technologies, but unevenly. Black churches in particular use all of these technologies less often than do white congregations. There is a digital divide even within the religious world.

It is not surprising that congregations, like everyone else, are embracing these new technologies. I expect these numbers to climb even higher in the coming years, probably reaching the saturation point before too long. The important question here is not whether congregations will continue to embrace the latest information technology—they will—but how the technology will shape congregations. Will it make congregations more efficient and effective, or will it impose new costs without providing clear benefits? Will it change how people choose congregations? Will it change how congregations operate? It is too soon to answer these questions definitively.[6]

Increased informality in worship is a fourth congregational trend evident since 1998. The NCS asked thirteen questions about each congregation's most recent main worship service in all three NCS waves. For each worship practice, if there is change since 1998 it is toward informality. Figure 5.4 shows the changes. More worship is characterized by drum playing, jumping or shouting or dancing, raising hands in praise, applause, calling out amen, and the use of visual projection equipment. (The visual projector change is repeated from figure 5.3 since it involves both technology and worship.) The consistent pattern is impressive.[7]

This trend toward informality is not occurring at the same pace and in the same way within every religious group. Most of it is among white Protestants. Catholic churches have seen only their use of visual projection equipment and drums rise. And black Protestant churches showed little change in any of these worship practices, mainly because they have had high levels of most of these practices throughout this period. At least 80 percent of

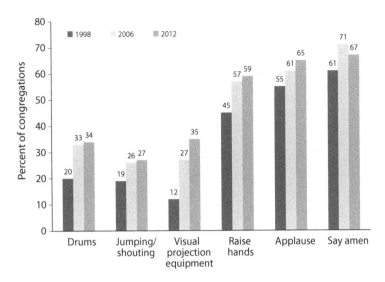

Figure 5.4. Growing Informality of Worship. Source: National Congregations Study

black churches indicated applause, jumping or dancing, spontaneously saying amen, and raising hands in praise in each survey year.

Still, there is a fairly general trend here, probably reflecting a broader trend in American culture toward informality. People dress more informally than they once did at work and social events as well as at worship services. When talking with each other, even with people we do not know well, we are less likely to use titles like Mr., Mrs., Doctor, Professor, or, for that matter, Reverend, Pastor, Father, or Rabbi. We are more likely to use first names, or even nicknames, even when children address adults. It makes sense

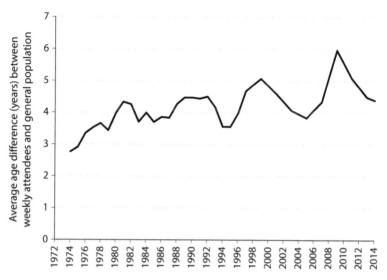

Figure 5.5. Aging Religious Service Attendees. Source: General Social Survey

that worship within an increasingly informal culture would become increasingly informal.

I return to GSS data to document a fifth trend within congregations: people in the pews are getting older. (As we'll see in chapter 6, the same is true for clergy.) Figure 5.5 shows the difference in average age between the overall adult population and adults who say they attend religious services at least weekly. The line creeps up—slowly but surely. Older people long have been over-represented in American congregations, but this over-representation has been exacerbated lately. In the 1970s frequent attendees were about three years older, on average, than the general population; today they are about five years older. People are living longer, and the U.S. adult population as a whole has grown older during this period, but the religiously active population has aged even faster. The average adult in the United States who attends religious services frequently is now fifty-one years old.[8]

A sixth change in congregations is their increasing acceptance of gays and lesbians. Greater acceptance of gays and lesbians is of course one of the most well-known public opinion shifts in recent years. This change also has occurred at a fast pace within religious congregations. The 1998 NCS did not ask about this, but the 2006 and 2012 NCS surveys asked congregations whether an openly gay or lesbian couple in a committed relationship would be permitted to be full-fledged members of the congregation, and whether such people would be permitted to hold all volunteer leadership positions open to other members. Figure 5.6 shows the trend. In just six years, the number of congregations whose leaders said that gays and lesbians could be full-fledged members increased from 37 to 48 percent. The number of congregations whose leaders said that no volunteer leadership positions were closed to gays and lesbians increased from 18 to 26 percent.

There are substantial differences in this trend across religious traditions. In contrast to the aggregate trend, for example, there seems to be less acceptance of gays and

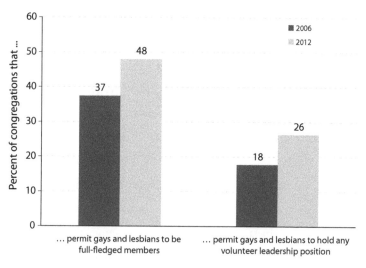

Figure 5.6. Increasing Acceptance of Gays and Lesbians by Congregations. Source: National Congregations Study

lesbians among Catholic churches in 2012 than there was in 2006. The number of Catholic parishes whose leaders said that gays and lesbians could be full-fledged members decreased from 74 to 53 percent. The number of Catholic parishes whose leaders said that no volunteer leadership positions were closed to gays and lesbians declined from 39 to 26 percent. This decline may reflect a backlash among some Catholic Church leaders against the legalization of gay marriage, a backlash evident in well-publicized instances of long-term teachers in Catholic schools losing their jobs, and long-term members denied communion, after marrying a same-sex partner. This result should not be interpreted as declining acceptance of gay and lesbian members and volunteer leaders among the Catholic rank and file, who, in line with national public opinion trends, have become more accepting of homosexuality.

Although more white conservative Protestants churches expressed acceptance of gay and lesbian members in 2012 than in 2006 (increasing from 16 to 24 percent), there was no increase in acceptance of gay or lesbian leaders (only 4 percent in 2012) within these churches. But the increased acceptance of gays and lesbians among black Protestant churches, white liberal churches, and non-Christian congregations were large enough to offset these patterns and produce an aggregate change that is remarkably large for just a six-year period.[9]

Overall, the changes evident within congregations mirror demographic and cultural changes in the American population as a whole. Only when it comes to the aging of their people are congregations on the leading edge of a demographic trend.

Earlier in this chapter I documented the declining size of the average congregation. A seventh congregational trend returns to the subject of size, but this time to focus on increasing concentration rather than declining average size. Most congregations are small, but most people are in large congregations. The median congregation has fewer than a hundred regular participants, but the median attendee is in a congregation with four hundred regular participants. Even though there are relatively few large congregations, these large congregations contain a disproportionate share of the religiously active population. The biggest 1 percent of Protestant churches, for example, contain approximately 20 percent of all the people, money, and staff. The biggest 7 percent contain half of all the people, money, and staff. People and resources are heavily concentrated in the biggest churches. This has been true of American religion for a long time, but there is a new twist: religious concentration is intensifying. More and more people are concentrated in the very largest congregations.

The most obvious sign of this trend is the increasing number of very large Protestant churches across the country, but this trend goes beyond proliferating megachurches. Data limitations make it difficult to assess whether or not this is happening within American Catholicism—and it does not seem to be happening among synagogues. But across the Protestant spectrum there are more very big churches. This might not be surprising for denominations that grew since the 1970s, such as the Southern Baptist Convention or the Assemblies of God, but the same trend also is evident in declining denominations. The number of very large churches also increased within the Episcopal Church, the Evangelical Lutheran Church in America, and the United Methodist Church, among others.[10]

It is not just that there are more megachurches. The very biggest churches also have become even larger. Interestingly, however, the churches at the top of the heap constantly change. Yesterday's biggest churches are not today's biggest churches. And this has been true for at least a hundred years. Across all the denominations I have examined, and across the entire twentieth century, the half-life of being one of the twenty biggest churches in your denomination is twenty to thirty years. Roughly speaking, if you look at the twenty biggest churches in a given year, only half of them are still on that list twenty years later, only one-quarter are still on the list forty years later, and only one-tenth are still on the list sixty years later. It is not that these very large churches shrink dramatically after reaching the top, although some do. Rather, the biggest churches of the moment generally reach that pinnacle by growing very fast, but they are then overtaken by a new cohort of churches that have caught that decade's cultural wave and ridden it quickly to the top, and then those churches are overtaken by the next wave, and on and on.

There are more very large churches, and the largest churches are bigger than before, but the key development is that people are increasingly concentrated in the very largest churches. Figure 5.7 tells the story. It shows the percent of people in the largest 1 percent of churches in eleven denominations, seven of which are tracked from early in

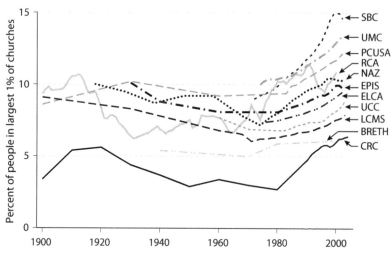

Figure 5.7. Increasing Concentration in American Protestantism. Note: The Assemblies of God trend is similar but it is more
dramatic and is not shown here because including it would
make it difficult to see the trends in the other denominations.
SBC = Southern Baptist Convention; UMC = United Method-
ist Church; PCUSA = Presbyterian Church (U.S.A.); RCA =
Reformed Church in America; NAZ = Church of the Nazarene;
EPIS = Episcopal Church; ELCA = Evangelical Lutheran Church
in America; UCC = United Church of Christ; LCMS = Lutheran
Church–Missouri Synod; BRETH = Church of the Brethren;
CRC = Christian Reformed Church in North America. Source:
Author's calculations from denominational data

the twentieth century to the beginning of the twenty-first
century.[11]

This is an astonishing picture because *every* denomination shows the same pattern of steadily—in some cases
rapidly—increasing concentration from 1970 to the present,

with no end in sight to this trend. Denominations vary in how concentrated they are, but all of them show the same trend toward increasing concentration since about 1970.

Note the overall shape of all the lines on this graph.[12] Concentration everywhere decreased until about 1970, after which it started to increase, again everywhere. The slight decrease between 1900 and 1970 is interesting, but I want to emphasize the dramatic increase since 1970: in every denomination on which we have data, people are becoming increasingly concentrated in the very largest churches, and this is true for small and large denominations, for conservative and liberal denominations, for growing and declining denominations. In some denominations, the largest 1 percent of churches includes those with only five hundred or so attendees on an average weekend. This is much smaller than the stereotypical megachurch, but part of the message here is that we should understand megachurch proliferation as one manifestation of a much broader phenomenon: churchgoers are increasingly concentrated in the very largest churches.[13]

Explaining this concentration trend is more difficult than establishing it. As we saw in chapter 4, religious service attendance did not increase during this period, so concentration has not increased because megachurches have figured out how to attract the "unchurched." Suburbanization surely is part of the story, but American society became steadily suburbanized throughout the twentieth century, with the fastest suburbanization occurring between 1945 and 1970, whereas the religious concentration trend began rather suddenly after 1970. Cultural, economic, and technological changes all may play a role, but it is difficult to say definitively what is behind this trend.[14]

Whatever is driving it, the movement of people into the largest congregations represents a significant change in American religion's social organization. This concentration trend is so strong that the average person is attending a larger congregation in 2012 than he or she attended in 1998 even though the size of the average congregation has declined somewhat since then. The median number of regularly participating adults in the average person's congregation increased from 275 in 1998 to 280 in 2006, and increased again to 301 in 2012. The median attendance at all weekend worship services at the average person's congregation increased from 325 in 2006 to 400 in 2012. Both of these things—the average person is participating in a larger congregation while the average congregation is shrinking— are happening at the same time because the churchgoing population has become more concentrated in larger congregations. Moreover, people in a larger congregation typically both give less money to it and participate less in its life. Ironically, far from representing any kind of resurgence in American religious involvement, proliferating megachurches may be contributing to its decline.[15]

6 | Leaders

It is more difficult to track change among religious leaders than among the population at large because we do not have an ongoing survey of American clergy. Nevertheless, I can document several important changes, including the declining attractiveness of religious leadership as a career choice, alterations in the social characteristics of clergy, and the public's declining confidence in religious leaders. All things considered, it seems that religious leaders have lost ground on several fronts.

There are clear signs that a career in religious leadership is less attractive than it used to be, especially among young people. Figure 6.1 shows the declining percentage of college freshmen saying that being a clergyperson is their expected

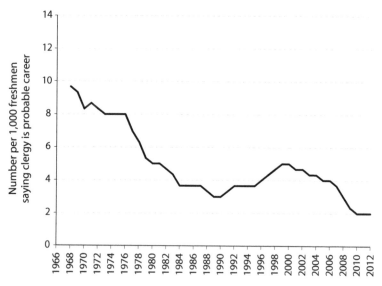

Figure 6.1. Declining Attractiveness of Religious Leadership to College Freshmen. Source: College Freshman Surveys, Higher Education Research Institute

occupation. About 1 percent (10 in 1000) of college freshmen expected to become clergy in the 1960s, declining rapidly to about 0.4 percent (4 in 1000) in the 1980s, and then declining more slowly to about 0.2 percent (2 in 1000) today. That means that the level of interest in a religious career among today's college freshmen is one fifth of what it was in 1970. This decline continues a very long-term trend. At the time of the Civil War, about 20 percent of college graduates became clergy, declining to 6 percent by 1900.[1]

Declining interest in a career might not be a problem for a professional group if the quality of those who pursue the career remains high. It is difficult to track trends in the talent and skill of those who become clergy, but scattered evidence suggests that interest in a religious career also has declined among the most academically talented. Of all individuals taking Graduate Record Examinations (GREs), the number saying they were headed to seminary declined 20 percent between 1981 and 1987. Moreover, the average verbal and analytical GRE scores of prospective seminary students declined during the 1980s, a decade in which average scores rose for all test takers. Prospective seminary students scored significantly lower than national averages on the quantitative and analytical sections of the GRE, although only male prospective Master of Divinity students scored lower than the national average on the verbal section of the test.[2]

Members of Phi Beta Kappa and Rhodes Scholars are a more select group than all those who take GREs, but a similar trend is evident among both of these groups. Four percent of Phi Beta Kappa members who graduated from college in the late 1940s became clergy, dropping to 2 percent for early 1970s college graduates and to 1 percent for early 1980s college graduates. Eight percent of American Rhodes Scholars in 1904–9 became clergy, dropping to 4 percent in 1955–59 and 1 percent in 1975–77. None of the 128 Rhodes Scholars in 2006–9 or the 255 in 2014–16 said that they aspired to be a clergyperson. Over this same period the flow of these academic stars into business, law, and medicine either increased or remained stable, though the proportion pursuing careers in higher education also declined. Neither GRE scores nor career choices of Phi Beta Kappa members or Rhodes Scholars are definitive measures of the average talent level of America's clergy, and many gifted individuals continue to become clergy. Still, it is noteworthy that all of these measures, however imperfect, point to declining interest in a religious career among the most intellectually talented.[3]

It is tempting to conclude from all this that the quality of religious leadership has declined in recent decades, but that would be going too far. None of the developments I describe speaks directly to the quality of religious leadership. Performance on the GRE may not be a good indicator of quality religious leadership. Drawing fewer people from the intellectual elite does not imply declining average quality. And attracting fewer college students to a profession does not necessarily imply a decline in average talent within the occupation. More fundamentally, we have no good way to assess leadership quality in the realm of religion. I would hesitate to even attempt such an assessment, in part because religious groups differ in the kinds of training, skills, and personal characteristics they think make for quality leaders. Some groups value religious zeal in clergy more highly than formal education. Another reason not to pronounce a decline in quality religious leadership is that, when it comes to formal education, clergy are better trained than ever. Today, about half of clergy who lead congregations have a graduate degree—the highest percentage since the American Revolution. Still, the signs are clear that interest in a religious career has declined among American young people in general and among the most intellectually elite young people in particular.[4]

One consequence of the declining interest in religious leadership among young people is the rather rapid aging of the American clergy in recent decades. This aging trend has been abetted by what seems to be increasing interest in religious leadership among middle-aged people looking for a second career. This aging trend is evident among seminary populations, where the average age of seminarians increased from twenty-five in 1962 to thirty-five in 1999. And it is evident in congregations. Only 35 percent of today's congregations are led by someone who is less than fifty years old, down from 48 percent in 1998. The American population as a whole is aging, but the clergy are aging faster. Between 1998 and 2012, the average age of the twenty-five-and-older American population increased by two years, from forty-seven to forty-nine. Meanwhile, the average age of sole or senior pastors increased five years, from fifty in 1998 to fifty-five in 2012. This aging is happening across the religious spectrum, though it is happening faster for Catholic and liberal Protestant churches than for others.[5] (The churchgoing

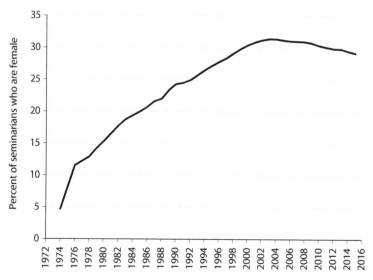

Figure 6.2. Increasing Presence of Women in Seminaries. Source: Yearbooks and data tables, Association of Theological Schools

population also is aging faster than the population as a whole, a trend I described in chapter 5.)

The influx of women is another major recent demographic trend for clergy. Figure 6.2 shows the increasing presence of women in seminaries. In 1972 only 5 percent of students enrolled in Master of Divinity programs were female. That increased steadily until it peaked at 31.5 percent in 2002, declining slightly since then. In 1970 only 3 percent of clergy in the United States were female; 16 percent were female in 2014. Since female clergy still are more likely to be assistants and associates rather than head clergy in congregations, only 11 percent of all congregations are led by women. Other predominantly male occupations also saw an increasing female presence over this period. Indeed, even though the feminization of the American clergy is a significant trend, the entrance of women into the clergy lags behind their entrance into medicine and law. Today about one-third of doctors and lawyers are women.[6]

The influx of women is related to the aging trend among clergy, since women are over-represented among those who become clergy later in life or as a second career. The average age at ordination for male clergy in 2001 was thirty-one; for women it was thirty-eight.[7]

Religious groups vary widely, of course, in their openness to female clergy. Some groups have none, while approximately 30 percent of churches within the most liberal Protestant denominations now are led by women. As the overwhelmingly male older cohorts of clergy are replaced by more female younger cohorts, we can expect the national percentage of female clergy to continue to increase slowly, but it probably will peak well below the 30 percent female mark that seminaries already have reached. And perhaps this trend provides another reason to refrain from concluding that clergy are, on average, less talented than they used to be, since female prospective seminary students outperform male prospective seminary students on the GRE.[8]

I turn now from the characteristics of religious leaders themselves to the public's confidence in those leaders. The

General Social Survey (GSS) has tracked public confidence in institutional leaders by asking people this question: "I am going to name some institutions in this country. As far as the people running these institutions are concerned, would you say you have a great deal of confidence, only some confidence, or hardly any confidence at all in them?" People then are read a list of institutions, including "organized religion." We do not know exactly which religious leaders people have in mind when they answer this question. We do not even know whether they are thinking about local leaders or national leaders. Probably people do not answer this question with a specific local or national leader in mind. It seems more likely that they answer in terms of their overall opinion about the category of religious leaders in general.

Whatever people are thinking when they answer this question, the trend in figure 6.3 is unmistakable. Americans have less confidence in religious leaders than they once did. The graph shows this trend both for all adults and for those who say they attend religious services at least once per month. Between 1973 and 2014, the number of people with a great deal of confidence in religious leaders declined from about 35 to about 20 percent. Confidence levels are higher among regular attendees than among the general public, but the trend is the same.

Religious leaders are not the only ones in whom the public has lost confidence in recent decades, as revealed

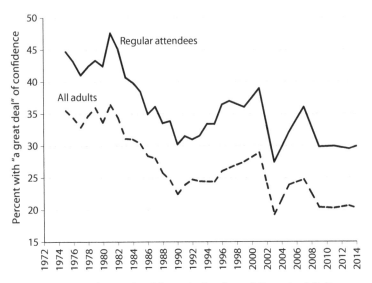

Figure 6.3. Declining Confidence in Leaders of Organized Religion. Source: General Social Survey

when the GSS asks people how much confidence they have in the leaders of a dozen other institutions. Levels of public confidence vary quite substantially across these types of institutions. Leading the pack in 2014 was the military, with 51 percent of people saying they have a "great deal of confidence" in military leaders. The other institutions, in order of public confidence, were: the scientific community (42 percent), medicine (38 percent), education (25 percent), U.S. Supreme Court (24 percent), organized religion (20 percent), major companies (19 percent), banks and financial institutions (15 percent), organized labor (12 percent), the executive branch of the federal government (11 percent), television (10 percent), the press (8 percent), and, bringing up the rear, Congress (6 percent). In addition to being the institution enjoying the greatest degree of public confidence, the military also is the only one of these institutions in which confidence has increased over this period. Confidence has declined in most other spheres while it held steady in just a few.

Religious leaders are not the only leaders in whom the public has lost confidence, but confidence in religious leaders has declined faster than confidence in the leaders of other institutions. Figure 6.4 tells the basic story. Combining the 1973–83 surveys, 34 percent of people, on average, expressed a great deal of confidence in the leaders of religious organizations, compared to only 28 percent, on average, expressing a great deal of confidence across all of the other institutions about which they were asked. Combining the 2004–14 surveys, only 22 percent expressed a great deal of confidence in religious organizations—about the same percentage expressing a great deal of confidence, on average, in the other kinds of institutions. In the 1970s religious leaders inspired somewhat greater public confidence than did leaders of other institutions, but their relative position has declined. People now express as low a degree of confidence in religious leaders as they do in leaders of other major institutions.

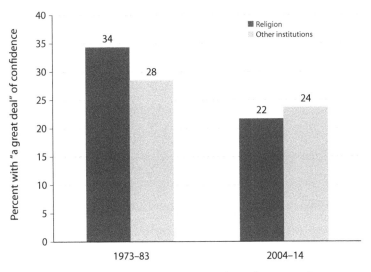

Figure 6.4. Declining Confidence in Leaders of Organized Religion and Other Institutions. Source: General Social Survey

Figure 6.3 shows a sudden drop between 2000 and 2002 in the percentage of people expressing a great deal of confidence in religious leaders. While most short-term blips or dips in trend lines could be read as random fluctuation in the data, I think this sudden drop represents a real change. Twenty-nine percent of people said they had a great deal of confidence in 2000, dropping to 19 percent in 2002. This is one of the largest two-year drops in confidence for any of the dozen institutions over the thirty-six years of the survey. It is comparable in magnitude to the sudden drop in confidence in banks and financial institutions caused by the 2008 global financial crisis.[9]

I think this crash in public confidence in religious leaders represents a real change because it exactly corresponds to a wave of negative national publicity about child sexual abuse by Catholic priests. Media reports about abusive Catholic priests had been appearing on and off since the late 1980s, but a firestorm of negative publicity was set off in January 2002, when the *Boston Globe* began a series of articles on the situation in the Boston archdiocese. These articles were distinctive in part because they emphasized Catholic leaders' irresponsible handling of abusive priests in a way that had not been emphasized before, and it was this leadership failure that reverberated throughout the country. The concomitant drop in public confidence evident in the 2002 survey seems unlikely to be a coincidence. Confidence in religious leaders, like confidence in other kinds of leaders, has eroded slowly but steadily since the 1970s, but it also nosedived as the Catholic abuse scandals became widely known in 2002. Confidence in religious leaders bounced back in 2004, but not to previous levels.[10]

Overall, it would be difficult to look at these trends and conclude that the past several decades have been good ones for religious leaders. The underlying trends are slow and, except for the Catholic child abuse scandal, nothing dramatic has occurred. So I would not say that religious leadership faces a time of acute crisis. I would say, however, that the broad picture portrays a professional group that has lost ground in recent decades when it comes to its reputation, social prominence, and attractiveness as a career choice for young people.[11] These trends are long-term, and it is difficult to see how they might be reversed.[12]

7 | Liberal Protestant Decline

The decline of liberal Protestant denominations is one of the best-known religious trends of the past several decades, but it often is misunderstood. Contrary to what many believe, this decline has not occurred because people have been leaving more liberal denominations in droves to join more conservative religious groups. Nor does the decline of liberal denominations mean that liberal religious ideas are waning. Indeed, as a set of ideas, religious liberalism steadily has gained ground in the United States, whatever the fate of the denominations most closely associated with it.

When thinking about religious differences in the United States, people naturally think first about differences between

Protestants, Catholics, Jews, and, more recently, Muslims, Hindus, Buddhists, and others. Another kind of fault line, however, runs *within* these religious groups: the division between liberals and conservatives. The "liberal" and "conservative" labels are somewhat tired and imprecise, and the specific disagreements between liberals and conservatives vary across religious groups and change over time. But there is no better way to capture an important division within every religion between those inclined to adapt their religion to a changing world and those inclined to resist such adaptation. There is no such thing as a religious group that never adapts to changes in the world; all religious groups selectively adapt, changing some beliefs and practices while maintaining others. There is a difference in spirit, however, between those within a religious group who welcome opportunities to adapt religious ideas and practices to cultural change and those who resist such opportunities. The 1880s split between Conservative and Reform Judaism, Pope Pius X's 1907 condemnation of modernism, the 1920s conflicts between fundamentalist and modernist Protestants, and the 1960s Catholic debates and reforms associated with Vatican II are only the best-known manifestations of longstanding liberal-conservative divisions among Protestants, Catholics, and Jews.[1]

This liberal-conservative division within religious groups always has existed to some degree, but through the 1950s and into the 1960s it seemed a less important axis of religious difference in the United States than the traditional differences between Protestants, Catholics, and Jews. The most famous sociological book about American religion published in the 1950s was tellingly titled *Protestant, Catholic, Jew*. And in 1961, the first major book using survey data to analyze religious differences in politics, economics, and family life compared what were considered the four major socio-religious groups at that time: white Protestants, white Catholics, black Protestants, and Jews.[2]

The American religious landscape looks different in the twenty-first century. We now usually distinguish among seven major socio-religious groups: white liberal Protestants, white conservative Protestants, black Protestants, Catholics, Jews, others (a catchall group including Mormons and Eastern Orthodox Christians as well as Muslims, Hindus, and Buddhists), and those with no religious affiliation.[3] These categories have expanded partly because the number of people in the United States who are neither Christian nor Jewish or claim no religious affiliation has increased. But it also is now necessary to split white Protestants into liberal and conservative camps, because liberal and conservative Protestant denominations followed dramatically different trajectories in recent decades: liberal denominations declined while conservative ones grew or held steady. These different trajectories have lent new importance to the long-standing liberal-conservative divide among Protestants.

In chapter 2, I documented the declining proportion of Americans who are Protestant without distinguishing between liberal and conservative Protestants. American Protestantism has declined, however, almost entirely because more liberal Protestant denominations have declined, and in this chapter I focus on the contrasting fortunes of liberal and conservative Protestant denominations. The liberal-conservative division is not limited to Protestantism, but its vagaries are more apparent among Protestants because the many different Protestant denominations can be divided roughly into these two camps, and their fortunes tracked. I limit my attention to predominantly white Protestant denominations because the different trajectories of liberal and conservative denominations are most apparent there.[4]

Within Protestantism, the liberal-conservative distinction captures differences in views about the Bible, attitudes about adapting religious traditions to cultural change, and opinions about the value of working with other religious groups and secular institutions to solve social problems. More liberal or mainline denominations interpret the Bible in light of the historical and social conditions in which it was written, and they express more openness to other religions and the secular world. More conservative or evangelical groups insist that the Bible's authority cannot be qualified by historical or cultural insights and tend to see other religions and secular institutions as targets of conversion rather than as partners in efforts to make a better world. The liberal or mainline denominations are the inheritors of a religious tradition, perhaps reaching its peak in the Social Gospel movement at the beginning of the twentieth century, encouraging wide-ranging institutional engagement between religious organizations and the world. Conservative or evangelical Protestant denominations are the inheritors of a religious tradition that discouraged such institutional engagement in favor of evangelism and an emphasis on individual morality rather than social reform or social service.

Figure 7.1 documents the shifting center of gravity within American Protestantism from more liberal or mainline (sometimes now called old line) denominations to more conservative or evangelical denominations. This figure is based on the self-reported denominational affiliations of General Social Survey respondents. People who say they are Protestant are asked for their specific denomination, and these denominations are divided into two groups based on their teaching about the Bible and their stance toward other religious groups and secular institutions and culture. The largest group in the liberal or mainline category is the United Methodist Church. Other sizable groups in that

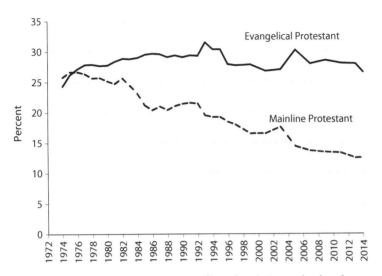

Figure 7.1. Percent of Americans Affiliated with Evangelical and Mainline Protestant Denominations. Source: General Social Survey

category include American Baptist Churches in the U.S.A., Episcopal Church, Evangelical Lutheran Church in America, Presbyterian Church (U.S.A.), and United Church of Christ. The largest group in the conservative or evangelical category is the Southern Baptist Convention. Other sizable groups in that category include Assemblies of God, Lutheran Church–Missouri Synod, and Seventh-day Adventist. People who say they are nondenominational also are classified as evangelical, as are people who say they are simply Christian.

It is important to keep in mind that people are not categorized as liberal or conservative in figure 7.1 based on their own religious beliefs or their own levels of religious activity or commitment. Rather, individuals are categorized based on the official positions taken by their denomination. This figure does not tell us about recent trends in what individuals believe about the Bible, engagement with the secular world, or anything else. There are people within conservative denominations who do not read the Bible literally, and there are people within more liberal denominations who do. This figure simply reflects changes in the extent to which people consider themselves part of a denomination that itself leans in a more conservative or more liberal direction.[5]

The trend is striking. Since 1972, the percentage of Americans affiliated with theologically more liberal, mainline denominations has steadily declined, while the percentage affiliated with more conservative, evangelical denominations increased slightly until the early 1990s and has remained stable since then. By 2014 almost twice as many people claimed affiliation with conservative denominations as with theologically more liberal ones: 25 percent compared to 13 percent.

What explains this growing size gap between evangelical and mainline white Protestants? Four factors can be identified. First, it is commonly believed that this growing gap results from people fleeing liberal denominations for more conservative churches. This is part of the story, but only part. There was a slightly increased flow of people from mainline to evangelical denominations from the 1970s to the 1980s. In the 1970s, 12 percent of people raised in a mainline denomination shifted to a more conservative denomination as an adult. That increased to 16 percent in the 1980s and has held steady at about that rate since then.[6] Conservative churches have benefited from a backlash against liberalizing changes in personal sexual morality, especially the greater acceptance of premarital sex and, more recently, increased tolerance of homosexuality. By emphasizing a traditional sexual morality that seems under fire, evangelical churches provide a refuge for people who dislike these cultural changes. This emphasis helps them hold on to the people they already have. To the extent that evangelical churches draw people from more liberal denominations, they attract those who like this emphasis on traditional sexual norms. But we should not overstate the magnitude of movement from more liberal to more conservative denominations. Today, more people raised in a mainline church become religiously unaffiliated than become evangelical.[7]

A second factor is often overlooked: differential fertility has produced approximately 80 percent of the diverging fortunes of liberal and conservative Protestant churches. For much of the previous hundred years, women affiliated with conservative Protestant denominations have borne one child more on average than those affiliated with more moderate and liberal denominations. One additional child may not sound like much, but over several generations that is a lot more people.[8]

Third, the flow of people between liberal and conservative denominations has changed in another way: fewer people switch from evangelical to mainline churches than did so in the past. This is a more important development than the slightly increased flow in the other direction. In the not-too-distant past, conservative denominations lost many more people to liberal denominations than they do now. Upward social mobility was a big reason for this flow of people in the liberal direction. Among upwardly mobile people who were raised as conservative Protestants, 29 percent of those born before 1931 switched to a more liberal denomination as an adult. Looking at people born after 1950, only 11 percent of upwardly mobile conservative Protestants switched to a mainline denomination. Conservative denominations have firmly established themselves as respectable, middle-class groups. People in more liberal, mainline denominations still have more education and income, on average, than those in conservative denominations, and upwardly mobile evangelicals still are more likely to switch to a liberal denomination than evangelicals who are not upwardly mobile. But in vast swathes of middle- and upper-middle-class America there no longer is any social stigma attached to being a conservative Protestant. Consequently, upward social mobility no longer prompts switching from being, say, Baptist to being Presbyterian as much as it did in the past. The pews of more liberal churches are emptier now partly because a steady influx of upwardly mobile former evangelicals has been stemmed.[9]

It's not just that conservative Protestant denominations lose fewer of their upwardly mobile young people to liberal denominations. A fourth dynamic behind the contrasting trajectories of liberal and conservative denominations is that conservative Protestants lose fewer of their youth to the ranks of the unaffiliated. Every group is losing increasing numbers of young people who leave their denomination and don't affiliate with another, but conservative denominations lose fewer. Looking at people born since 1960, conservative Protestant denominations lost 13 percent of their youth to the ranks of the unaffiliated, compared to 17 percent for more liberal denominations. This may not seem like a big difference until we realize what it means: in recent years conservative denominations have been losing 25 percent fewer young people from every cohort as it comes of age. This retention difference probably exists because evangelical families place more emphasis on religion than mainline families do, and conservative churches involve young people in a denser social web of youth groups, church camps, and church-based socializing, all of which increase the chances that a young person will remain in the fold as an adult.

In sum, evangelical and conservative churches and denominations have been doing better than liberal denominations in recent decades, but not primarily because people switched from liberal to conservative churches. Evangelical denominations now hold a somewhat larger share of the American population and a much larger share of the Protestant population mainly because their families produced more children than did mainline families and because they did a better job of retaining the people they already had. This is a story of liberal losses more than one of conservative gains.

It seems likely that the trajectories of conservative and liberal Protestant denominations will not be as different over the next several decades as they have been over the past several ones. Conservative denominations are losing their competitive edge. Evangelical birthrates remain higher than liberal birthrates, but they are nevertheless declining, narrowing the fertility gap between liberal and conservative Protestants. Conservative Protestant denominations continue to lose fewer people to the ranks of the unaffiliated than do more liberal denominations, but they are losing more than before. And there now seems to be a backlash to the backlash that kept culturally conservative people in more conservative denominations in the 1970s and 1980s.

Americans' views about sexual morality, especially young people's views of homosexuality, have grown ever more liberal in recent years. Conservative Protestant churches' appeal still rests in part on strong resistance to homosexuality and strong insistence on sexual abstinence for the unmarried, but there is a shrinking pool of people attracted to making these stances central to their religious identity. Indeed, several major conservative denominations have reported membership losses since 2007.[10]

Whatever the future trajectories of liberal and conservative Protestant denominations, the decline of liberal denominations does not mean the decline of liberal religious ideas. Recall some of the facts about Americans' religious beliefs that I highlighted in earlier chapters: three-quarters of Americans say a religion other than their own offers a true path to God; 67 percent say that religions other than their own can lead to eternal life; and only about 1 in 3 Americans believes that the Bible is the "actual word of God and is to be taken literally, word for word." Moreover, almost half of religiously affiliated people say that their church or denomination should adjust its traditional beliefs and practices or adopt modern beliefs and practices in light of new circumstances, and half of all Christians say that some non-Christian religions can lead to eternal life. There are predictable differences among religious traditions in these numbers, but even a majority of white evangelicals say that many religions can lead to eternal life and there is more than one true way to interpret the teachings of their religion. If this isn't theological liberalism, what is? Liberal denominations have suffered decline, and relatively few people will admit to being a religious liberal. At the same time, however, Americans' increasing endorsement of theological liberalism's core tenets—appreciating other religions, adjusting traditional belief and practice to modern circumstances, rejecting biblical literalism—shows that religious liberalism is a more potent cultural presence than many realize.[11]

8 | Polarization

Actively religious Americans are more politically and socially conservative than less religious Americans. Active participants support more restrictions on legal abortion, endorse more traditional gender roles, and vote Republican more often than less religious people. These differences have existed at least since the 1970s, but some of them have increased since then, creating a tighter link between religiosity and some kinds of political and social conservatism. This development has changed religion's place in American culture and politics, but not to an extent that amounts to culture war—yet.

Figure 8.1 shows the trend in the correlation between religious service attendance and two measures of political

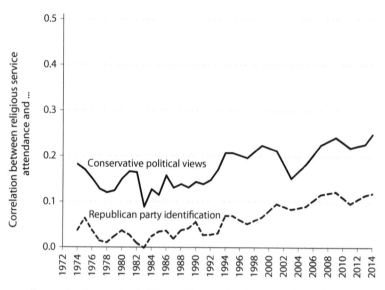

Figure 8.1. Increasingly Strong Connection between Attendance and Political Conservatism. Source: General Social Survey

conservatism: how liberal or conservative a person's political views are and how strongly he or she identifies with the Republican Party.[1] The correlation between attendance and political conservatism always is above zero, meaning that throughout this period more religiously active people also tend to be more politically conservative.[2] Most importantly, however, the correlation has strengthened in recent decades, especially after 1992.

Figure 8.2 conveys this trend's meaning and magnitude. In the 1970s, 19 percent of respondents who attended religious services at least weekly said that their political views

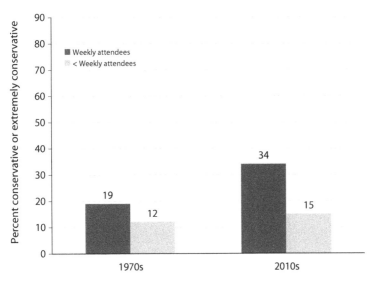

Figure 8.2. Tighter Connection between Attendance and Political Conservatism. Source: General Social Survey

were conservative or extremely conservative, compared to 12 percent of less frequent attendees. Combining the 2010–14 surveys, 34 percent of weekly attendees said they were conservative or extremely conservative, compared to only 15 percent of less frequent attendees. Religiously active people were only a little bit more conservative than others in the 1970s; today they are more than twice as likely as others to say they are very conservative. Over recent decades, infrequent religious service attendees have become only slightly more politically conservative while weekly attendees have become much more conservative. The gap between these groups has widened considerably. That wider gap—which political scientists call the "God gap"—is the essence of religiosity's tighter link to political conservatism.[3]

The picture is similar for political party identification. In the 1970s, 9 percent of weekly attendees stated that they were strong Republicans, compared to 7 percent of less frequent attendees. The comparable numbers in the 2010s are 17 percent for weekly attendees and 8 percent for others. Weekly attendees have moved from being nearly indistinguishable from others in their political party affiliations to being twice as likely as others to call themselves strong Republicans. This is a significant change.

The trend is similar when it comes to some kinds of social conservatism: attitudes about abortion and sex. The abortion trend is particularly interesting. The General Social Survey (GSS) asks people if they support legal abortion in any of seven situations: if there is a strong chance of serious defect in the baby, if the woman is married and does not want any more children, if her own health is seriously endangered by the pregnancy, if the family has very low income and cannot afford any more children, if she became pregnant as a result of rape, if she is not married and does not want to marry the man, and if the woman wants an abortion for any reason.[4] Opposing legal abortion in any of these situations is strongly correlated with religious service attendance, but these correlations have become stronger in

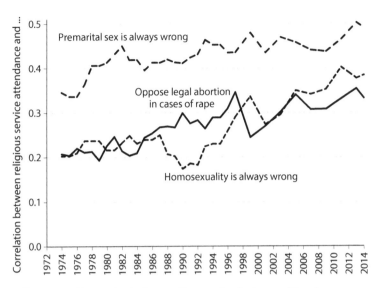

Figure 8.3. Increasingly Strong Connection between Attendance and Social Conservatism. Source: General Social Survey

recent decades for only two situations: abortion in the case of rape and in the case of serious fetal defect.

Figure 8.3 shows the trend in the correlation between attendance and several types of social conservatism, including opposing legal abortion in cases of rape. The abortion correlation has steadily increased since the 1970s. Being religiously active is now more tightly connected to opposing legal abortion in cases of rape than it was in the 1970s. Figure 8.4 displays relevant percentages. In the 1970s, 29 percent of weekly attendees opposed legal abortion in cases of rape, compared with 12 percent of less frequent attendees.

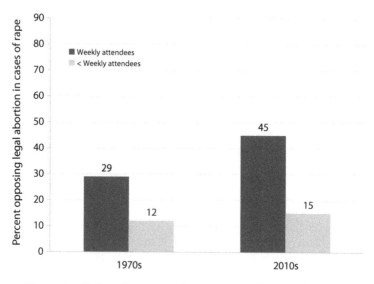

Figure 8.4. Tighter Connection between Attendance and Attitude about Abortion in Cases of Rape. Source: General Social Survey

In the 2010s, 45 percent of weekly attendees opposed legal abortion in this situation, compared with only 15 percent of less frequent attendees. The trend is similar for abortion in cases of serious fetal defect.

Like the trend in political conservatism, the attitude gap between weekly and infrequent attendees has widened substantially when it comes to abortion in cases of rape and serious fetal defect, with a substantially greater number of frequent attendees opposing such practice. By contrast, the gap between the attitudes of frequent attendees and those of others is *not* widening when it comes to most other situations in which a woman might seek an abortion. Rather, the most religiously active people have increased their attitudinal distance from the rest of the population only with respect to two situations in which there is overwhelming popular support for legal abortion.[5]

On the issues of both political identity and abortion, the population at large grew more conservative and the correlation with attendance at worhip services increased because the most religious people became especially conservative. Something different happened with other attitudes. Figure 8.3 also shows trends in the correlations between attendance and attitudes about premarital sex and homosexuality.[6] Like political conservatism and opposing abortion in cases of rape or serious defect, disapproval of premarital sex and of homosexuality became more tightly connected to religious service attendance over time. But figure 8.5 shows a very different dynamic behind the sexuality trends. In the 1970s, 85 percent of weekly attendees said that homosexuality is always wrong compared to 67 percent of infrequent attendees, while since 2010 the comparable numbers are 74 and 33 percent, respectively. Both the religious and the nonreligious have liberalized on this issue, but the less religious people have liberalized much faster. The picture is similar for attitudes about premarital sex. In the 1970s, 53 percent of weekly religious service attendees said that premarital sex is always wrong, compared to 22 percent of

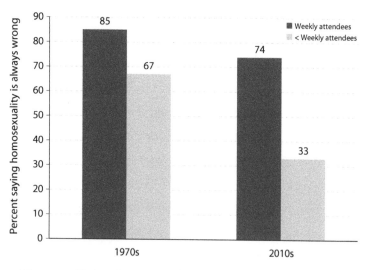

Figure 8.5. Tighter Connection between Attendance and Attitude about Homosexuality. Source: General Social Survey

infrequent attendees; the comparable 2010–2014 numbers are 48 percent and 11 percent, respectively. Both groups are more liberal on premarital sex today than they were in the 1970s, but less frequent attendees have become more liberal at a faster rate.[7]

Across these issue areas, the basic trend is clear: opinion differences line up with religious differences more than they did before. For political identification and attitudes about abortion in cases of rape or serious fetal defect, the connection between religious service attendance and conservatism is tighter because the most religious people became more conservative over time. For attitudes about homosexuality, the connection is tighter because, even though the most religious people are liberalizing on this issue, they are doing so more slowly than others. These very different dynamics both increase the attitudinal distance between the most and least religiously active people in the United States.

Why has this happened? The complexities make it difficult to answer this question definitively, but three things are clear. First, the decline of liberal Protestant denominations described in the previous chapter and declining religious service attendance among Catholics means that more of the most religiously active people in the United States are evangelical Protestants. In the 1970s, only about one-quarter of those who attended religious services at least weekly were in predominantly white evangelical Protestant denominations; today slightly more than 40 percent of weekly attendees are in those denominations.[8] The religiously active population is now more concentrated than it was before in the most politically and socially conservative religious groups, and that produces a tighter connection between attendance and political and social conservatism.

Figure 8.6 illustrates in a different way the increasing evangelical dominance of the religiously active population by showing that biblical literalism has increased among weekly attendees while decreasing among everyone else. In the 1980s, 48 percent of weekly religious service attendees said that the Bible is the literal word of God, compared to

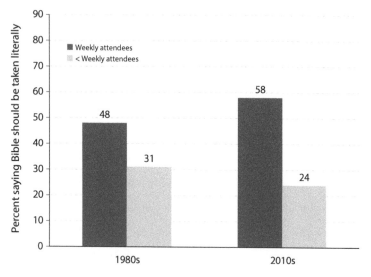

Figure 8.6. Tighter Connection between Attendance and Biblical Literalism. Source: General Social Survey

31 percent of less frequent attendees; the comparable 2010s numbers are 58 percent and 24 percent. The trend is similar, according to the GSS, when it comes to respondents having had a born-again experience.[9] Fifty-seven percent of 1990s weekly attendees said they were born again, compared to 29 percent of infrequent attendees; the comparable 2010s numbers are 66 and 30 percent. We do not see this trend when it comes to general sorts of belief and practice like believing in God or praying frequently. We see the trend only when it comes to believing in biblical inerrancy and saying you have been born again, because the trend reflects the increasing dominance of a specific type of conservative

evangelical Protestant theology among the churchgoing population.

Simply put, compared with earlier decades, more of today's actively religious people in the United States are evangelical Protestant, and this development has contributed to the increasingly tight connection between religiosity itself and some kinds of political and social conservatism. This development, by the way, also has produced a linguistic change, in that the word "Christian" is increasingly used in everyday speech and in the mass media to refer to a particular kind of Christian: an evangelical Protestant.

A second cause of the increasingly tight connection between religious service attendance and some kinds of social and political conservatism is that people have been changing their religion to match their political and social views. This may be surprising, since we tend to think of social and political views mainly flowing out of stable religious commitments rather than vice versa. But Americans frequently change their religious affiliations and their religious activity as their lives change. Marrying or divorcing, having children, and moving to a different part of the country are especially powerful causes of religious change. And it seems that Americans now also change their religious identities and activity in response to politics. Religiosity's tighter link with conservatism is not simply a matter of a stable group of religiously active people becoming more conservative (or becoming more liberal at a slower rate) compared to a stable group of less religious people. Conservatism and religiosity also align more closely because more conservative people have become more religious and less conservative people have become less religious. People changing their religious identity and practice to align more closely with their politics is more common than is generally appreciated.[10]

Third, the growing gap between the highly religious and the less religious has been driven by activists from both ends of the political spectrum who pushed political parties to emphasize issues with religious resonance and who pushed religious groups to emphasize politics. If the Republican and Democratic parties did not take clearly different stands on abortion, people would not choose between the parties based on their opinions about abortion. But once the parties made that issue central to their identities, people were more likely to vote for candidates who shared their views. From the other direction, if denominations or congregations did not emphasize their stands on abortion or homosexuality, people would not choose a denomination or congregation based on their views on these issues. But they will once religious groups make these issues central to their identities. When political leaders emphasize religion and religious leaders emphasize politics, people will more closely align their politics with their religion and their religion with their politics. This is why people now are more likely to use religion to sort themselves politically, and they are more likely to use politics to sort themselves religiously.[11]

The tighter connection between religiosity and political and social conservatism does not yet amount to true culture war between religious and secular people in the United States. I say this for four reasons. First, religion is not the only social characteristic that is more tightly connected to political conservatism now than it was before. The income gap between those voting Republican and those voting Democratic also has increased in recent decades, with higher-income people even more likely to vote Republican now than they were before. A gender gap also now exists: women vote Democratic at higher rates than men, something that was not true in the 1970s. This larger context, in which religion is just one axis of political and cultural division—and probably not the most important axis—makes me reluctant to declare that we now are completely divided on religious grounds.[12]

Second, neither the religiously active nor the religiously inactive are unified in their political and cultural views. On the contrary, opinions vary within both groups. This internal variation means that many religiously active and inactive people share the same political and social views. In a group of a hundred regular churchgoers, for example, thirty-four are very conservative politically and forty-five oppose legal abortion even in cases of rape. In a group of a hundred people who are not regular attendees, fifteen are very conservative and fifteen oppose abortion even in cases of rape. These are real and important differences in the center of gravity within each group, but those differences should not obscure the fact that most people in both groups are not very conservative, and that most people in both groups support legal abortion in cases of rape. Differences of opinion *within* groups help to prevent differences of opinion *between* groups from developing into true culture war.

Third, recall that both the religiously active and the religiously inactive trend in the same direction on several key attitudes and political leanings, albeit at different rates. Even the most actively religious people have become more liberal in their attitudes about homosexuality. When two groups change in the same direction but at different rates, they can become more distant from each other for a time, but distance created in this way seems less like polarization than it would if the two groups moved in opposite directions. Attendees and nonattendees are heading in opposite directions only when it comes to *religious* conservatism.

Fourth, although—and perhaps because—religion has become more tightly connected with political and social conservatism, the public increasingly *dis*approves of politicized religion. Figure 8.7 shows that the number of people who strongly agreed that "religious leaders should *not* try to

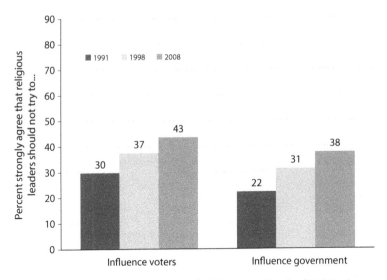

Figure 8.7. Increasing Disapproval of Religious Leaders' Political Involvement. Source: General Social Survey

influence how people vote in elections" increased from 30 percent in 1991 to 37 percent in 1998, and increased again to 44 percent in 2008. The number who strongly agreed that "religious leaders should *not* try to influence government decisions" increased from 22 percent in 1991 to 31 percent in 1998, and increased again to 38 percent in 2008. According to Gallup polls, agreement that organized religion should have less influence in this nation increased from 22 percent in 2001 to 29 percent in 2011. It is difficult to know if this increasing disapproval of religion's public presence is a reaction to political activism that was explicitly proclaimed, and sometimes celebrated, as religiously motivated. Still, these trends suggest that the American public has become less enamored of some kinds of explicit religious involvement in politics.[13]

All in all, then, the increasing attitudinal distance between the most and least religiously active people in U.S. society does not yet amount to culture war. That characterization seems misplaced when the religious cleavage is one of several cross-cutting social cleavages, when there is much overlap between the most and the least religious people in their opinions even on the most prominent hot button issues, when even the most religious people are liberalizing on homosexuality, and when Americans are increasingly wary of attempts to exploit for political purposes the attitudinal differences between religious and nonreligious people.

Still, we should not be sanguine about widening differences of opinion between the more religious and the less religious on key political and cultural issues. The alignment that exists today does not yet look like true culture war between the more and the less religious segments of American society. That could change, however, if political leaders continue to push the more religious and the less religious further apart politically, and if religious leaders continue to push political liberals and conservatives further apart religiously.

9 | Conclusion

The religious trends I have documented point to a straightforward general conclusion: *American religiosity has been declining for decades.* Not all of the changes I have discussed are about decline. There is more religious diversity, there are shifting fortunes for liberal and conservative Protestant denominations, and there are troubling signs about the state of religious leadership. Changes are occurring inside congregations, and there is a tighter connection between religious service attendance and political, social, and religious conservatism. There is more diffuse spirituality, though this phenomenon should not be mistaken for an increase in traditional religiosity. But a lot of the changes are about decline. Indeed, every indicator of traditional religious belief or practice is either stable or declining, and most are declining. The trend is toward less religion.

If religiosity is declining in the United States, why do people sometimes think it is holding steady, or even increasing?

Part of the answer lies in the still high levels of religious belief and practice in the United States, and the slowness of the decline. Americans remain very religious by world standards, and, as I have emphasized at several points in the preceding pages, the decline has been slow enough that only recently have we amassed enough data over a long enough time span to be able to see it clearly.

Another part of the answer lies in the increasingly tight connection between religiosity and political and social conservatism described in chapter 8. This is the social reality behind—and in part created by—the rise of the religious right and the subsequent politicization of religion in recent decades. This development increased religion's visibility in politics at every level even though there were no increases in Americans' actual religiosity.

Yet another part of the answer is the increasing concentration of churchgoers within very large churches. This shift, which I documented in chapter 5, increases religion's visibility—and possibly its social and political influence— even in the face of stable or declining religiosity among individuals. One 2000-person church is more visible than ten 200-person churches. One 2000-person church presents a more attractive audience for a politician than ten 200-person churches. The pastor of a 2000-person church gets an appointment with the mayor more easily than the pastors of 200-person churches. Increasing religious concentration, in other words, can create the impression that more people are turning to religion when what really is under way is a change in religion's social organization.

Organizational concentration can lead to a real increase in the social and political influence of religious congregations and their leaders, if only because it creates more very large congregations and more leaders of very large congregations with whom to contend. But we should not mistake this change in social organization for an increase in the underlying levels of religious belief and practice in the society. There is no such increase. People sometimes think there is because they mistakenly equate more visible religion with more religion.

It is difficult to see how the trends I have described could amount to good news for American religious institutions, but what about for American society as a whole? My assessment is mixed. Increased tolerance of, even appreciation for, religions other than one's own, described in chapter 2, is good news for our increasingly pluralistic society. Together with the fact that our families and friendship circles are more religiously diverse than before, this cultural trend will help prevent religious differences from degenerating into incivility or hostility. Countering this positive trend, however, is the increasing attitudinal difference between the more religious and the less religious. As I noted at the end of chapter 8, we do not yet have dangerous polarization between the more and the less religious segments of American society, but that could change if leaders and activists continue to push people to align their religion and their politics ever more closely. It would be ironic and unfortunate if Americans' increasing appreciation for religions other than their own becomes overwhelmed by increasing hostility between the more and the less religious.

Polarization aside, people who do not care about American religious institutions for their own sake still might be concerned that the hollowing out of some traditional religious beliefs and practices—alongside a tentative increase in a generic spirituality—could point to a future in which American religiosity may be less grounded in institutions. Despite continuing high levels of religious belief and some kinds of practice, religious institutions may or may not find ways for people to express their religiosity through face-to-face gatherings and local organizations to the same extent as they have in the past. If half of all the social capital in America—meaning half of all the face-to-face associational activity, personal philanthropy, and volunteering—happens through religious institutions, the vitality of those institutions influences more than American religious life. Weaker religious institutions would mean a different kind of American civic life.[1]

The religious trends I have documented in this book have not occurred in isolation. Recent waves of immigration contribute to religious diversity and to increased acceptance of that diversity. The century-long movement of the American population from rural areas into cities and suburbs and decades-long increases in educational attainment levels also have shaped religious belief and practice. Changes in American family life, such as higher divorce rates, later age at first marriage, lower fertility, declining percentages of two-parent-plus-children households, and the movement of women into the paid labor force, have affected American religious life and institutions. The rapid diffusion of computer technologies across American society influences both private and corporate expressions of religion in ways we have only begun to understand. And declining involvement in religious congregations reflects broader trends in civic engagement and involvement in other kinds of voluntary associations. I touched on some of this context in this book, but here I want to emphasize that these long-term, largely demographic, forces have shaped and will continue to shape American religion more profoundly than the latest religious scandal, conflict, or innovation. Such high-profile events may affect religious belief and behavior in the short term, but they rarely have a lasting impact. Even the uptick in religious service attendance that followed the September 11 terrorist attacks disappeared within a few weeks.[2] Understanding and explaining American religious trends requires seeing how religion is shaped by social and demographic processes that play out over decades.

Before we attempt to understand and explain religious change, however, we need to know what is and is not changing. I hope this book helps meet that need.

Notes

1 Introduction

1. Overstated attendance was first documented in C. Kirk Hadaway, Penny Long Marler, and Mark Chaves, "What the Polls Don't Show: A Closer Look at U.S. Church Attendance," *American Sociological Review* 58 (1993): 741–52. Subsequent studies have confirmed it. I discuss this phenomenon in chapter 4. For overviews and explanations of international differences in religiosity, see Pippa Norris and Ronald Inglehart, *Sacred and Secular: Religion and Politics Worldwide, Second Edition* (New York: Cambridge University Press, 2011); Tom W. Smith, "Religious Change around the World," General Social Survey Cross-National Report No. 30 (Chicago: National Opinion Research Center, 2009); David Voas, "The Rise and Fall of Fuzzy Fidelity in Europe," *European Sociological Review* 25 (2009): 155–68; and Philip S. Brenner, "Cross-national Trends in Religious Service Attendance," *Public Opinion Quarterly* 80 (2016): 563–83.

2. Brooks E. Holifield, "Towards a History of American Congregations," 23–53, in *American Congregations, Volume 2: New Per-*

spectives in the Study of Congregations, ed. James P. Wind and James W. Lewis (Chicago: University of Chicago Press, 1994), 24.

3. Three recent general assessments of religious change in the United States are *U.S. Public Becoming Less Religious* (Washington, D.C.: Pew Research Center, 2015); Robert D. Putnam and David E. Campbell, *American Grace: How Religion Divides and Unites Us* (New York: Simon & Schuster, 2010); and Claude S. Fischer and Michael Hout, *Century of Difference: How America Changed in the Last One Hundred Years* (New York: Russell Sage Foundation, 2006), chapter 8. These works explore several of the same themes and trends I discuss in this book. For a thoughtful interpretation of contemporary American religion, see Alan Wolfe, *The Transformation of American Religion: How We Actually Live Our Faith* (Chicago: University of Chicago Press, 2003). For a still relevant assessment of major changes in American religion since 1945, see Robert Wuthnow, *The Restructuring of American Religion: Society and Faith since World War II* (Princeton: Princeton University Press, 1988).

4. For years in which they overlap and on subjects they have explored in common, surveys by Gallup and by the Pew Research Center paint a picture of change that is very similar to the picture painted by the GSS. This kind of agreement among different data sources increases confidence that we are seeing real trends. See Appendix C of the Pew Research Center's 2015 report, "U.S. Public Becoming Less Religious," for a comparison of trends across these three data sources.

5. Unless otherwise noted, all numbers mentioned in this book are from the GSS or the NCS, and all percentages or mean differences to which I call attention are statistically significant at least at the 0.05 level. The GSS data are weighted by the variable WTSSALL, and they take into account the black oversamples in 1982 and 1987. Unless otherwise noted, trend lines in the figures are smoothed by interpolating data points between survey years and calculating

three-year moving averages. See the GSS and NCS websites for more information about these surveys: www.gss.norc.org and www .soc.duke.edu/natcong. For more methodological detail about many of the trends discussed in this book, see Mark Chaves and Shawna Anderson, "Continuity and Change in American Religion, 1972–2008," in *Social Trends in the United States, 1972–2008: Evidence from the General Social Survey*, ed. Peter V. Marsden (Princeton: Princeton University Press, 2011); and "Changing American Congregations: Findings from the Third Wave of the National Congregations Study," *Journal for the Scientific Study of Religion* 53 (2014): 676–686. The 2016 GSS data were released too late to be included in this book, but I have examined the 2016 results, and nothing in them requires changing any of my interpretations or conclusions.

6. The GSS asked about Bible reading in 1988 and 1998, with no change in reported levels, and it asked about belief in heaven or hell three times between 1991 and 2008, again with no change in reported levels. Pooling the GSS surveys that asked these questions, we find that 31 percent of Americans said they read the Bible at least once a week, 86 percent said they definitely or probably believed in heaven, and 73 percent said they definitely or probably believed in hell. I conclude that levels of Bible reading and believing in heaven and hell remain stable through 2014 because the Pew Research Center asked similar questions in their 2007 and 2014 surveys, and they saw no change. See their 2015 report, "U.S. Public Becoming Less Religious," pp. 17, 53, and 55.

7. The evidence for long-term decline in belief in God is from Tom W. Smith, "Religious Change around the World," p. 3 and table 2.

2 Diversity

1. "Religion Reported by the Civilian Population of the United States: March 1957," *Current Population Reports: Population Characteristics*. Series P-20, no. 79, released 2 February (United States Department of Commerce, Bureau of the Census, 1958).

2. Fischer and Hout, *Century of Difference*, 193–94.

3. For more on religious "nones," see Barry A. Kosmin and Ariela Keysar, *American Nones: The Profile of the No Religion Population: A Report Based on the American Religious Identification Survey 2008* (Hartford, Conn.: Program on Public Values, Trinity College, 2009, available at www.americanreligionsurvey-aris .org); Michael Hout and Claude S. Fischer, "Explaining Why More Americans Have No Religious Preference: Political Backlash and Generational Succession, 1987–2012," *Sociological Science* 1 (2012): 423–47; Chaeyoon Lim, Carol Ann McGregor, and Robert D. Putnam, "Secular and Liminal: Discovering Heterogeneity among Religious Nones," *Journal for the Scientific Study of Religion* 49 (2010): 596–618; Elisabeth Drescher, *Choosing Our Religion: The Spiritual Lives of America's Nones* (New York: Oxford University Press, 2016); and Christel J. Manning, *Losing Our Religion: How Unaffiliated Parents Are Raising Their Children* (New York: New York University Press, 2015).

4. The American Community Survey (ACS) is an ongoing survey of the American population conducted by the U.S. Census Bureau. ACS results can be found at http://factfinder.census.gov.

5. The immigration facts are from Richard Alba and Victor Nee, *Remaking the American Mainstream: Assimilation and Contemporary Immigration* (Cambridge: Harvard University Press, 2003), 181–82; and Guillermina Jasso, Douglas S. Massey, Mark P. Rosenzweig, and James P. Smith, "Exploring the Religious Preferences of Recent Immigrants to the United States: Evidence from the New Immigrant Survey Pilot," 217–53 in *Religion and Immigration: Christian, Jewish, and Muslim Experiences in the United States*, ed. Yvonne Yazbeck Haddad, Jane I. Smith, and John L. Esposito (Walnut Creek, Calif.: AltaMira, 2003).

6. For more on the size of the Muslim, Buddhist, and Hindu populations in the United States, see Tom W. Smith, "Religious Diversity in America: The Emergence of Muslims, Buddhists, Hindus,

and Others," *Journal for the Scientific Study of Religion* 41 (2002): 577–85; Tom W. Smith, "The Muslim Population in the United States: The Methodology of Estimates," *Public Opinion Quarterly* 66 (2002): 404–17; and *America's Changing Religious Landscape* (Washington, D.C.: Pew Research Forum, 2015).

7. For more on Protestant decline, see Tom W. Smith and Seokho Kim, "The Vanishing Protestant Majority," *Journal for the Scientific Study of Religion* 44 (2005): 211–23.

8. Putnam and Campbell, *American Grace*, 526–27. For more on religious and other kinds of intermarriage, see Michael J. Rosenfeld, "Racial, Educational and Religious Endogamy in the United States: A Comparative Historical Perspective," *Social Forces* 87 (2008): 1–31.

9. The presidential voting numbers are from a 2015 Gallup poll reported in Frank Newport, "Six in 10 Americans Would Say 'Yes' to Muslim President," available at www.gallup.com. The "three-quarters of Americans say" and the Muncie numbers are reported in Fischer and Hout, *Century of Difference*, 192, 200, and 341, n41. The Muncie numbers are originally from Theodore Caplow, Howard M. Bahr, Bruce A. Chadwick, and Dwight W. Hoover, *All Faithful People: Change and Continuity in Middletown's Religion* (Minneapolis: University of Minneapolis Press, 1983). The 67 percent figure is from the Pew Research Forum's 2015 report, *U.S. Public Becoming Less Religious*. For broad discussions of religious pluralism, see Diana Eck, *A New Religious America: How a "Christian Country" Has Now Become the Most Religiously Diverse Nation on Earth* (San Francisco: Harper San Francisco, 2001); and Robert Wuthnow, *America and the Challenges of Religious Diversity* (Princeton: Princeton University Press, 2005).

10. GSS respondents sometimes are asked about their feelings toward Protestants, Catholics, Jews, and Muslims using the following item:

I'd like to get your feelings toward groups that are in the news these days. I will use something we call the feeling thermometer, and here is how it works. I'll read the names of a group and I'd like you to rate that group using the feeling thermometer. Ratings between 50 degrees and 100 degrees mean that you feel favorable and warm toward the group. Ratings between 0 degrees and 50 degrees mean that you don't feel favorable toward the group and that you don't care too much for that group.

In 2004, the most recent year in which this question was asked on the GSS, the mean temperature ratings were 66 for Protestants, 63 for Catholics, 61 for Jews, but only 48 for Muslims. A 2006 national survey that asked this same question found a similar pattern (Putnam and Campbell, *American Grace*, 505).

11. For details about public attitudes toward Muslim Americans, see Costas Panagopoulos, "Arab and Muslim Americans and Islam in the Aftermath of 9/11," *Public Opinion Quarterly* 70 (2006): 608–24; Chelsea E. Schafer and Greg M. Shaw, "Tolerance in the United States," *Public Opinion Quarterly* 73 (2009): 404–31; and Christopher Bail, *Terrified: How Anti-Muslim Fringe Organizations Became Mainstream* (Princeton: Princeton University Press, 2015), p. 113. For a social and attitudinal portrait of American Muslims, see Jen'nan Read, "Muslims in America," *Contexts* 7 (Fall 2008): 39–43.

12. The slight decline from 32 to 30 percent of predominantly white congregations having some Latino presence is not statistically significant. Moreover, no decline is even hinted at when we look at the percentage of *people* in predominantly white congregations with some Latino presence rather than the percentage of such *congregations*. The percentage of religious service attendees in predominantly white congregations with some Latino presence was 49 in 1998, 56 in 2006, and 57 in 2012.

13. The 1.7-to-4 percent trend is from Sangyoub Park, "Who and What You Are," *Contexts* 8, no. 4 (2009): 64–65. The other intermarriage numbers are from Jeffrey S. Passel, Wendy Wang, and

Paul Taylor, "Marrying Out: One-in-Seven New U.S. Marriages is Interracial or Interethnic," a research report issued by the Pew Research Center (Washington, D.C., 2010).

14. For more detail about correlations between worship style and education, see Mark Chaves, *Congregations in America* (Cambridge: Harvard University Press, 2004), chapter 5.

15. For more on ethnic diversity within churches see Michael Emerson, *People of the Dream: Multiracial Congregations in the United States* (Princeton: Princeton University Press, 2006); Korie L. Edwards, *The Elusive Dream: The Power of Race in Interracial Churches* (New York: Oxford University Press, 2008); and Korie L. Edwards, Brad Christerson, and Michael O. Emerson, "Race, Religious Organizations, and Integration." *Annual Review of Sociology* 39 (2013): 211–28. For more on immigration's impact on American congregations, see R. Stephen Warner and Judith G. Wittner, eds., *Gatherings in Diaspora: Religious Communities and the New Immigration* (Philadelphia: Temple University Press, 1998); and Wendy Cadge and Elaine Howard Ecklund, "Immigration and Religion," *Annual Review of Sociology* 33 (2007): 359–79.

16. Scholars have debated whether religious diversity enhances or diminishes religious vitality. For overviews of that debate, see Mark Chaves and Philip S. Gorski, "Religious Pluralism and Religious Participation," *Annual Review of Sociology* 27 (2001): 261–81, and Daniel V. A. Olson, Miao Li, Paul Perl, and David Voas, "Does Religious Diversity Affect Religious Commitment: Some New Answers to an Old Question," (paper presented at the annual meetings of the Society for the Scientific Study of Religion, Boston, 2013).

3 Belief

1. Smith, "Religious Change around the World," p. 3 and table 2C.

2. Here and throughout, I calculate percentages concerning education only for people who are at least 24 years old. Including people between the ages of 18 and 24 distorts the picture because

too many 18- to 24-year-olds are on their way to a bachelor's degree even if they do not have one yet.

3. Claude Fischer and Michael Hout point out in *Century of Difference* (208–9) that over the twentieth century belief in inerrancy declined most among people without a high school diploma. So the overall decline in belief in inerrancy is not wholly explained by the increasing proportion of people who graduated from college or, in an earlier time, by increases in high school attendance and graduation.

4. For more on trends in belief in the afterlife, see Andrew M. Greeley and Michael Hout, "Americans' Increasing Belief in Life after Death: Religious Competition and Acculturation," *American Sociological Review* 64 (1999): 813–35.

5. For more on the spiritual-but-not-religious phenomenon, see Penny Long Marler and C. Kirk Hadaway, "'Being Religious' or 'Being Spiritual' in America: A Zero-Sum Proposition?" *Journal for the Scientific Study of Religion* 41 (2002): 289–300; Linda M. Chatters, Robert Joseph Taylor, Kai M. Bullard, and James S. Jackson, "Spirituality and Subjective Religiosity among African Americans, Caribbean Blacks, and Non-Hispanic Whites," *Journal for the Scientific Study of Religion* 47 (2008): 725–37; Courtney Bender, *The New Metaphysicals: Spirituality and the American Religious Imagination* (Chicago: University of Chicago Press, 2010); and Nancy T. Ammerman, "Spiritual but not Religious? Beyond Binary Choices in the Study of Religion," *Journal for the Scientific Study of Religion* 52 (2013) 258–78.

6. A classic discussion of how religious belief can remain high even though involvement declines is provided by Grace Davie in *Religion in Britain Since 1945: Believing Without Belonging* (Cambridge: Blackwell, 1994).

4 Involvement

1. The American Time Use Survey (ATUS) numbers are calculated from ATUS data available at www.bls.gov/tus/. These calculations use the "attending religious services" code (140101) for reports

on Sunday activities. As noted in the main text, incorporating people who attend on other days (but not also on Sundays), which is not possible to do with ATUS data, would add only about two percentage points to the attendance rate. I am grateful to Simon Brauer for performing these calculations.

2. Exaggerated religious service attendance was first documented by C. Kirk Hadaway, Penny Long Marler, and Mark Chaves in "What the Polls Don't Show: A Closer Look at U.S. Church Attendance." A symposium on the subject appeared in the February 1998 issue of the *American Sociological Review*. One of the articles in that symposium focused on the time diary approach: Stanley Presser and Linda Stinson, "Data Collection Mode and Social Desirability Bias in Self-Reported Religious Attendance," *American Sociological Review* 63 (1998): 137–45. For more on religious service attendance overreporting, see Philip S. Brenner, "Exceptional Behavior or Exceptional Identity? Overreporting of Church Attendance in the U.S.," *Public Opinion Quarterly* 75 (2011): 19–41; "Testing the Veracity of Self-Reported Religious Practice in the Muslim World," *Social Forces* 92 (2014): 1009–37; and Philip S. Brenner and John DeLamater, "Measurement Directiveness as a Cause of Response Bias: Evidence from Two Survey Experiments," *Sociological Methods & Research* 45 (2016): 348–71.

3. The GSS weekly attendance rates are calculated by translating each attendance category into the probability of attending in any given week. For example, saying you attend less than once a year gives you a .01 chance of attending on any given week, saying you attend once a month gives you a .23 probability, and saying you attend every week gives you a .99 probability. The earliest time diary number is from the University of Maryland's 1992–94 Time Use Survey, reported in Stanley Presser and Linda Stinson, "Data Collection Mode and Social Desirability Bias in Self-Reported Religious Attendance." The GSS lines do not look qualitatively different if the unusually religious 1972 GSS is dropped.

4. The population growth rate is from the U.S. Census Bureau, Population Division, *Table 3. Estimates of Resident Population Change for the United States, Regions, States, and Puerto Rico and Region and State Rankings: July 1, 2015 to July 1, 2016 (NST-EST2016-03)*, released in December 2016. I calculated the declining absolute number of religious service attendees using U.S. population totals and GSS attendance rate estimates for recent years.

5. Claude Fischer and Michael Hout conclude that "the key trend in attendance over the last half-century or more has been the decline in Catholic attendance to the level of that of mainline Protestants" (*Century of Difference*, 207).

6. Figure 4.2 combines results from two sets of questions, asked in various years, about parents' religious service attendance when the respondent was a child. People with no father present when they were growing up are excluded from these calculations, and so the sharp decline in fathers' attendance is not an artifact of increasing divorce or more single-mother households. Reliability checks show that these trends are not produced by people reporting a more religious childhood as they age.

7. Presser and Stinson, "Data Collection Mode and Social Desirability Bias"; Sandra L. Hofferth and John F. Sandberg, "Changes in American Children's Time, 1981–1997," 193–229 in *Children at the Millenium: Where Have We Come From, Where Are We Going? Advances in Life Course Research*, ed. Timothy Owens and Sandra Hofferth (New York: Elsevier Science, 2001); and Robert Wuthnow, *After the Baby Boomers: How Twenty- and Thirty-Somethings Are Shaping the Future of American Religion* (Princeton: Princeton University Press, 2007), 53.

8. Figure 4.3 is a redrawing of figure 9 on page 1,542 of David Voas and Mark Chaves, "Is the United States a Counterexample to the Secularization Thesis?" *American Journal of Sociology* 121 (2016): 1517–56. The lines are smoothed using a three-survey moving average rather than a three-year moving average. That article

also contains similar graphs for religious affiliation and belief in God in the United States and other countries, and it contains the analysis showing that virtually all of the attendance decline since the 1980s is produced by cohort replacement. The discussion in this paragraph and the next is based on that article's findings.

9. The never married numbers are from Wendy Wang and Kim Parker, *Record Share of Americans Have Never Married* (Washington, D.C.: Pew Research Center, 2014). The childlessness numbers are from *Childlessness Falls, Family Size Grows among Highly Educated Women* (Washington, D.C.: Pew Research Center, 2015). For more on the connection between religious involvement and family structure, see Penny Edgell, *Religion and Family in a Changing Society* (Princeton: Princeton University Press, 2006).

5 Congregations

1. The best estimate of the number of congregations in the United States (384,000) is from Simon Brauer, "How Many Congregations Are There? Updating a Survey-Based Estimate," *Journal for the Scientific Study of Religion* 56 (2017): forthcoming. The large research literature on congregations includes the work of Nancy Tatom Ammerman, *Pillars of Faith: American Congregations and Their Partners* (Berkeley: University of California Press, 2005); Mark Chaves, *Congregations in America* (Cambridge: Harvard University Press, 2004); Penny Edgell Becker, *Congregations in Conflict: Cultural Models of Local Religious Life* (New York: Cambridge University Press, 1999); Katie Day, *Faith on the Avenue: Religion on a City Street* (New York: Oxford University Press, 2014); Paul Numrich and Elfriede Wedam, *Religion and Community in the New Urban America* (New York: Oxford University Press, 2015); and Mark Mulder, *Shades of White Flight: Evangelical Congregations and Urban Departure* (New Brunswick, N.J.: Rutgers University Press, 2015).

2. The National Congregations Study, a survey of a nationally representative sample of religious congregations from across the

religious spectrum, was conducted in 1998 with 1,234 participating congregations, in 2006–7 with 1,506 congregations participating, and again in 2012 with 1,331 congregations. See note 5 in chapter 1 for more information about this study.

3. For more detail about these continuities see Brad R. Fulton, "Trends in Addressing Social Needs: A Longitudinal Study of Congregation-Based Service Provision and Political Participation," *Religions 7* (2016), 51; and Mark Chaves and Alison Eagle, *Religious Congregations in 21st Century America* (Durham: Duke University Department of Sociology, 2015), 16–17.

4. I focus on medians because the heavily skewed size distribution makes medians much more meaningful than means. Trends in the means of the logged variables show the same qualitative pattern. For four of these five items the downward trend is statistically significant at least as the .05 level. The trend in the logged mean of the total number of people associated in any way with the congregation does not reach statistical significance. For more details see Mark Chaves and Shawna Anderson, "Changing American Congregations." For corroborating evidence from a different data source, see David A. Roozen, *A Decade of Change in American Congregations, 2000–2010* (Hartford, Conn.: Hartford Institute for Religion Research, 2011).

5. A megachurch is commonly defined as "a Protestant church that averages at least two thousand total attendees in . . . weekend services" (Scott Thumma and Dave Travis, *Beyond Megachurch Myths: What We Can Learn from America's Largest Churches* [San Francisco: Jossey-Bass, 2007], xviii). It is, of course, arbitrary to use 2,000 attendees as a cut-off point, and in a world in which the median congregation has only 70 regular participants and only 7 percent of all congregations have more than 400 regular participants, Protestant churches should be considered very large even if they fall far short of 2,000 weekly attendees. For megachurch denominational affiliations, see ibid., 26–27. For the longer-term trend of

congregations spending more locally and giving less to their denominations, see John L. Ronsvalle and Sylvia Ronsvalle, *The State of Church Giving Through 2013: Crisis or Potential?* (Champaign, Ill.: empty tomb, inc., 2015), 18. They report that "benevolence" spending, which includes contributions to denominations as well as contributions to local charities and social ministries, declined from 21 percent of all congregational spending in 1968 to 15 percent in 2013. For a study showing the increasing presence of unaffiliated churches within one city, see Peter Dobkin Hall, "Vital Signs: Organizational Population Trends and Civic Engagement in New Haven, Connecticut, 1850–1998," in *Civic Engagement in American Democracy*, ed. Theda Skocpol and Morris P. Fiorina (Washington, D.C.: Brookings Institution; New York: Russell Sage Foundation, 1999), 211–48, especially 233. For information about a related phenomenon, the growth of "parachurch" organizations, see Christopher P. Scheitle, *Beyond the Congregation: Christian Nonprofits and the Parachurch Movement* (New York: Oxford University Press, 2010).

6. For more on congregations' technology use, see Scott Thumma, "Regularly Attending to Internet Altars: A New Look at the Use of the Internet by Churches," paper presented at the annual meeting of the Society for the Scientific Study of Religion, Portland, Ore., 2006, and Christopher P. Scheitle, "The Social and Symbolic Boundaries of Congregations: An Analysis of Website Links," *Interdisciplinary Journal of Research on Religion* 1 (2005): article 6, retrieved 1 April 2008, http//:www. religjournal.com.

7. Each of these trends except for applause is statistically significant at least at the .05 level, though some are significant only when the data are weighted to give the percentage of people in congregations with these practices rather than the percentage of congregations with each practice. I include applause in figure 5.4 anyway because what is impressive here is the consistent pattern across many distinct items, and applause fits that pattern.

8. Combining the 2010–14 General Social Surveys, the average age of adults who say they attend religious services at least weekly is 51 years.

9. Acceptance of gay and lesbian members among white liberal Protestant churches increased from 67 percent in 2006 to 76 percent in 2012; acceptance of gay and lesbian volunteer leaders increased from 53 to 63 percent. Among black Protestant churches, the increases were from 44 to 62 percent accepting gay and lesbian members and from 7 to 22 percent accepting gay and lesbian volunteer leaders. I hesitate to report numbers for non-Christian congregations because that is such a small and heterogeneous category in the NCS sample.

10. The facts in this and following paragraphs are from my research on concentration within American religion. For more details about that research, see Mark Chaves, "All Creatures Great and Small: Megachurches in Context," *Review of Religious Research* 47 (2006): 329–46.

11. A twelfth denomination, the Assemblies of God, shows the same trend. I do not include them in figure 5.7 because the concentration trend is most extreme among Assemblies congregations, and including them would make it difficult to see the trends within the other groups. Figure 5.7 is based on congregational size data gathered from denominations' annual reports. It is important to note that I have not cherry-picked just the denominations that show the same striking pattern. Neither Mormon wards nor Jewish synagogues show this trend, and the data we would need to assess whether or not something similar is happening within Catholicism do not exist. But every Protestant denomination I looked at shows this same pattern. See Chaves, "All Creatures Great and Small" for more details.

12. It is difficult to discern which lines in this figure correspond to which denominations. A color version of this figure is available from the author. Fortunately, the key point is how similarly shaped

all the lines are, which is why I include this black-and-white version here despite its visual limitations.

13. I have not tried to examine more recent data for all of these denominations, but I have done so for several of them. This spot checking suggests that the concentration trend has not yet peaked.

14. For more on megachurches, see Chaves, "All Creatures Great and Small"; Thumma and Travis, *Beyond Megachurch Myths*; Nancy L. Eiesland, *A Particular Place: Urban Restructuring and Religious Ecology in a Southern Exurb* (New Brunswick, N.J.: Rutgers University Press, 2000); Stephen Ellingson, *The Megachurch and the Mainline: Remaking Religious Tradition in the Twenty-First Century* (Chicago: University of Chicago Press, 2007); David A. Snow, James A. Bany, Michelle Peria, and James E. Stobaugh, "A Team Field Study of the Appeal of Megachurches," *Ethnography* 11 (2010): 165–88; and David Eagle, "Historicizing the Megachurch," *Journal of Social History* 48 (2015): 589–604.

15. For more on the relationship between congregational size and giving, see Chaves and Eagle, *Religious Congregations in 21st Century America*, 6–8. For more on the relationship between congregational size and involvement, see David Eagle, "Congregational Size and Frequency of Attendance: A Possible Pathway to Secularization," *Socius: Sociological Research for a Dynamic World* 2 (2015): 1–10.

6 Leaders

1. The college freshman trend is from Kevin Eagan, Ellen Bara Stolzenberg, Joseph J. Ramirez, Melissa C. Aragon, Maria Ramirez Suchard, and Cecilia Rios-Aguilar, *The American Freshman: Fifty-Year Trends, 1966–2015* (Los Angeles: Higher Education Research Institute, University of California, Los Angeles, 2016). Figure 6.1 includes data only through 2012 because in 2013 HERI changed the response options for the intended occupation question in a way that renders the percent choosing clergy incomparable to previous

years. The nineteenth-century numbers are from Bailey B. Burritt, *Professional Distribution of College and University Graduates*, U.S. Bureau of Education, Bulletin No. 19, Whole Number 491 (Washington, DC: Government Printing Office, 1912), 74–75. Burritt drew on alumni catalogs from thirty-seven colleges and universities.

2. Jerilee Grandy and Mark Greiner, "Academic Preparation of Master of Divinity Candidates," Ministry Research Notes: An ETS Occasional Report (Princeton, N.J.: Educational Testing Service, Fall 1990). To my knowledge this study has not been updated.

3. The Phi Beta Kappa numbers are from Howard R. Bowen and Jack H. Schuster, *American Professors: A National Resource Imperiled* (Oxford University Press, 1986), 224–28. The Rhodes Scholar numbers through the 1970s are my calculations using *A Register of Rhodes Scholars, 1903–1981* (Oxford: Alden Press, 1981). Information about the career aspirations of 2006–9 and 2014–16 Rhodes Scholars was taken from the scholar profiles at www.rhodes scholar.org. Several profiles evidence scholars' religious interests and commitments even though none aspire to professional religious leadership. I did not review the scholar profiles for the 2010–13 classes.

4. The long-term increase in clergy education is from E. Brooks Holifield, *God's Ambassadors: A History of the Christian Clergy in America* (Grand Rapids, MI: William B. Eerdmans Publishing Company, 2007), 332. For more about clergy education see Chaves and Eagle, *Religious Congregations in 21st Century America*, 18–19.

5. The seminary numbers are from Jackson W. Carroll, *God's Potters: Pastoral Leadership and the Shaping of Congregations* (Grand Rapids, Mich.: William B. Eerdmans, 2006), 72–73. The other numbers, as usual, are from the National Congregations Study (NCS) and the General Social Survey (GSS).

6. The seminary numbers are from Association of Theological Schools' reports and data tables available at www.ats.edu. The 1970 percentage of female clergy is from the 1970 U.S. Census; the

2014 percentages of female clergy, lawyers, and doctors are from the U.S. Census Bureau, 2014 American Community Survey, available at www.census.gov/people/io/publications/table_packages.htm. The percentage of congregations led by women is from the NCS.

7. Carroll, *God's Potters*, 69.

8. Combining NCS data from five of the more liberal Protestant denominations—United Methodist Church, Evangelical Lutheran Church in America (ELCA), Presbyterian Church (U.S.A.) (PCUSA), Episcopal Church, and United Church of Christ—26 percent of congregations were led by women in 2012. In 2015, 32 percent of ELCA congregations with a called pastor were led by women (personal correspondence, Kenneth Inskeep, Executive for Research and Evaluation, ELCA). And, including congregations with a female co-pastor but not including congregations led by commissioned lay people, 32 percent of PCUSA congregations were led by women in 2015 (personal correspondence, Perry Chang, Associate for Survey Research, PCUSA). Grandy and Greiner (ETS Occasional Report, Fall 1990) reported the gender differences in GRE scores.

9. In 2006, 30 percent of people said they had a great deal of confidence in the leaders of banks and financial institutions, but that plummeted to 19 percent in 2008 and to 11 percent in 2010.

10. The account of media coverage of the Catholic abuse crisis is drawn from Andrew Walsh, "The Scandal of Secrecy," *Religion in the News* 5 (Spring 2002). For more on this crisis, see Andrew M. Greeley, *Priests: A Calling in Crisis* (Chicago: University of Chicago Press, 2004). The GSS conducts its interviews in spring and summer, so it makes sense that a scandal that broke in January 2002 would affect responses to the 2002 survey.

11. Average clergy salaries have outpaced inflation in recent decades, but it is difficult to assess whether or not clergy have lost ground relative to salaries in other occupations. For relevant evidence see James Hudnut-Beumler, *In Pursuit of the Almighty's*

Dollar: A History of Money and American Protestantism (Chapel Hill: University of North Carolina Press, 2007); Becky R. McMillan and Matthew J. Price, *How Much Should We Pay the Pastor? A Fresh Look at Clergy Salaries in the 21st Century*, Pulpit & Pew Research Report No. 2. (Durham, N.C.: Duke Divinity School, 2003); and Cyrus Schleifer and Mark Chaves, "The Price of the Calling: Exploring Clergy Compensation Using Current Population Survey Data," *Journal for the Scientific Study of Religion* 55 (2016): 130–52.

12. For more on the history and current state of American clergy, see Carroll, *God's Potters*; Greeley, *Priests*; and Holifield, *God's Ambassadors: A History of the Christian Clergy in America*.

7 Liberal Protestant Decline

1. For more on the liberal-conservative divide in American religion, see William R. Hutchison, *The Modernist Impulse in American Protestantism* (Cambridge: Harvard University Press, 1976); Martin E. Marty, *Modern American Religion. Vol. 2. The Noise of Conflict, 1919–1941* (Chicago: University of Chicago Press, 1991); Wuthnow, *The Restructuring of American Religion*; John Seidler and Katherine Meyer, *Conflict and Change in the Catholic Church* (New Brunswick, N.J.: Rutgers University Press, 1989); Gene Burns, *The Frontiers of Catholicism: The Politics of Ideology in a Liberal World* (Berkeley: University of California Press, 1992); Jack Wertheimer, *A People Divided: Judaism in Contemporary America* (Boston: Brandeis University Press, 1997); and James K Wellman, Jr., *Evangelical vs. Liberal: The Clash of Christian Cultures in the Pacific Northwest* (New York: Oxford University Press, 2008).

2. Will Herberg, *Protestant, Catholic, Jew: An Essay in American Religious Sociology* (Garden City, N.Y.: Doubleday, 1955); Gerhard Lenski, *The Religious Factor: A Sociologist's Inquiry* (Garden City, N.Y.: Doubleday, 1961).

3. For more detail about this standard set of categories, especially concerning which Protestant denominations are classified as liberal and which as conservative, see Brian Steensland, Jerry Z. Park, Mark D. Regnerus, Lynn D. Robinson, W. Bradford Wilcox, and Robert D. Woodberry, "The Measure of American Religion: Toward Improving the State of the Art," *Social Forces* 79 (2000): 291–318.

4. Of course, there are African Americans and other ethnic minorities within predominantly white denominations. Indeed, as I documented in chapter 2, there are *growing* numbers of African Americans and other ethnic minorities within predominantly white churches.

5. I constructed these categories using a slightly modified version of the classification described in Steensland et al., "The Measure of American Religion." The trend lines take into account the 1984 change in the way the GSS classified people into denominations.

6. Mainline denominations also have lost entire congregations to more conservative denominations, such as when recent shifts in some denominations toward more openness to gays and lesbians in leadership positions produced a wave of congregational defections. Between 2009 and 2015, for example, the Evangelical Lutheran Church in America lost 688 churches and the Presbyterian Church (U.S.A.) lost 513—approximately 5 percent of the congregations in these denominations. Jack Marcum, "W(h)ither the Mainline? Trends and Prospects," *Review of Religious Research* 59 (2017): forthcoming.

7. This first factor is drawn from Putnam and Campbell, *American Grace*, 117–20. Unless otherwise noted, all numerical facts in this chapter are my calculations from GSS data.

8. This factor and the next two are drawn from Michael Hout, Andrew M. Greeley, and Melissa J. Wilde, "The Demographic Imperative in Religious Change in the United States," *American Journal of Sociology* 107 (2001): 468–500.

9. These numbers are for whites who were at least 25 years old at the time they were interviewed. Upwardly mobile respondents are those who have at least a bachelor's degree but whose fathers did not. The pattern is the same if I use mother's education, and it is the same if I define upward mobility more broadly as any increased level of schooling compared to one's father: graduating from high school if your father did not, receiving a two-year college degree if your father did not, and so on. The pattern also is the same if we limit attention to those at least 45 years old at the time they were interviewed.

10. The birth rate facts are from Hout et al., "The Demographic Imperative." The observation about a backlash to the backlash about liberalizing sexual morality is from Putnam and Campbell, *American Grace*, 120–33. The observation about increasing conservative losses to secularity is based on my analysis of GSS data. Martin E. Marty reported membership losses for the Southern Baptist Convention, the Lutheran Church–Missouri Synod, and the Presbyterian Church in America in "Decline in Conservative Churches," *Sightings* (emailed newsletter, 14 December 2009). His report is based on these denominations' official membership counts.

11. Sources for "three-quarters" and "67 percent" are given in note 9 of chapter 2. The biblical inerrancy trend is discussed in chapter 3. The "more than one true way to interpret" finding is from a 2007 survey conducted by the Pew Research Center. The other numbers in this paragraph are from the 2014 Pew survey also cited in note 9 of chapter 2. For more on the contrast between liberal Protestantism and cultural and organizational fortunes, see N. J. Demerath III, "Cultural Victory and Organizational Defeat in the Paradoxical Decline of Liberal Protestantism," *Journal for the Scientific Study of Religion* 34 (1995): 458–469; and David A. Hollinger, "After Cloven Tongues of Fire: Ecumenical Protestantism and the Modern American Encounter with Diversity," *Journal of American History* XCVIII (2011): 21–48.

8 Polarization

1. Here are the exact GSS questions: "We hear a lot of talk these days about liberals and conservatives. I'm going to show you a seven-point scale on which the political views that people might hold are arranged from extremely liberal to extremely conservative. Where would you place yourself on this scale?" (Figure 8.2 combines the sixth point on this scale, labeled "conservative," and the seventh point, labeled "extremely conservative." The fifth point on the scale is labeled "slightly conservative.") "Generally speaking, do you usually think of yourself as a Republican, Democrat, Independent, or what?" If Republican or Democrat: "Would you call yourself a strong (Republican/Democrat) or a not very strong (Republican/Democrat)?" If Independent, no preference, or other: "Do you think of yourself as closer to the Republican or Democratic party?" These questions produce a seven-point scale ranging from "strong Democrat" to "strong Republican."

2. The vertical axis on figures 8.1 and 8.3 is the Pearson product-moment correlation coefficient. The vertical axis runs in principle from −1.0 to +1.0 and represents the strength of the connection between frequent attendance and political conservatism. A zero on this scale would mean that there is no association whatsoever between attendance and political conservatism, indicating that religiously active people are no more or less conservative, on average, than others. A score of −1.0 would mean that more frequent attendees were always less conservative than others, while a score of +1.0 would mean that more frequent attendees were always more conservative.

3. The increasingly tight connection between religious service attendance and political conservatism is well documented and analyzed by political scientists. See, for example, John C. Green, *The Faith Factor: How Religion Influences American Elections* (Westport, Conn.: Praeger, 2007); Morris P. Fiorina, with Samuel J. Abrams and Jeremy C. Pope, *Culture War? The Myth of a Polarized*

America, 2nd ed. (New York: Pearson Longman, 2006); David E. Campbell, "The Young and the Realigning: A Test of the Socialization Theory of Realignment," *Public Opinion Quarterly* 66 (2002): 209–34; Putnam and Campbell, *American Grace*, chapter 11; and Andrew Gelman, *Red State, Blue State, Rich State, Poor State: Why Americans Vote the Way They Do* (Princeton: Princeton University Press, 2009), chapter 6. The trend is apparent in the American National Election Studies (ANES) as well as in the GSS. Fiorina et al. (*Culture War?*) using ANES data, also notice a qualitative change in 1992.

4. The GSS question wording is as follows: "Please tell me whether or not you think it should be possible for a pregnant woman to obtain a legal abortion if [fill in specific situation]."

5. Combining the 2010–14 surveys, here are the percentages of people who support legal abortion in each situation: woman's health is seriously endangered (87 percent); pregnancy as a result of rape (78 percent); strong chance of serious defect in the baby (74 percent); married and does not want any more children (47 percent); very low income and cannot afford any more children (45 percent); wants an abortion for any reason (44 percent); unmarried and does not want to marry the man (42 percent).

6. The GSS questions are as follows: "If a man and woman have sexual relations before marriage, do you think it is always wrong, almost always wrong, wrong only sometimes, or not wrong at all?" "What about sexual relations between two adults of the same sex. Do you think it is always wrong, almost always wrong, wrong only sometimes, or not wrong at all?"

7. Attitudes about euthanasia show a similar pattern: the overall trend is in a liberal direction, but the most religiously active people are liberalizing more slowly. In the 1970s, 58 percent of weekly attendees, compared to 32 percent of less frequent attendees, opposed legal euthanasia when requested by a terminally ill patient. The comparable numbers from the 2010s are 55 percent and 23 percent.

8. In the 1970s, 27 percent of people who said they attend services at least weekly were in predominantly white evangelical denominations, 21 percent were in the more liberal white mainline denominations, and 39 percent were Catholic. In the second decade of the twenty-first century, the comparable numbers are 43 percent evangelical, 12 percent liberal Protestant, and 24 percent Catholic. Filling out the rest of the picture in the 2010s, 11 percent of weekly attendees were black Protestants, 1 percent were Jewish, 7 percent were something other than Christian or Jewish, and 2 percent said they had no religious affiliation.

9. The born-again item reads as follows: "Would you say you have been 'born again' or have had a 'born again' experience—that is, a turning point in your life when you committed yourself to Christ?" The Bible item is the same one described in chapter 3. The Bible item was not asked in the GSS until 1984; the born-again item was not asked until 1988. The "1990s" born-again numbers include the 1988 survey.

10. As I noted in chapter 2, Claude Fischer and Michael Hout showed that the accelerated growth after 1990 in people saying they have no religion was driven by political liberals and moderates who were pushed to alter their religious identity by an uncomfortable association between religion and conservative politics. In *American Grace*, Robert Putnam and David Campbell showed that "some Americans make choices about their religion based on their politics" (434; see also 143–45). And Ziad W. Munson, in *The Making of Pro-Life Activists: How Social Movement Mobilization Works* (Chicago: University of Chicago Press, 2008), chapter 7, observed that anti-abortion activists commonly became more religious as a consequence of their activism.

11. For more on cultural polarization, culture war, and the complex sorting processes behind these trends, see Paul DiMaggio, John Evans, and Bethany Bryson, "Have Americans' Social Attitudes Become More Polarized?" *American Journal of Sociology* 102

(1996): 690–755; Rhys H. Williams, ed., *Cultural Wars in American Politics: Critical Reviews of a Popular Myth* (New York: Aldine de Gruyter, 1997); Fiorina et al., *Culture War?*; Fischer and Hout, *Century of Difference,* chapter 9; Delia Baldassarri and Andrew Gelman, "Partisans without Constraint: Political Polarization and Trends in American Public Opinion," *American Journal of Sociology* 114 (2008): 408–46; and Robert Putnam and David Campbell, *American Grace,* chapters 11, 12, and 14.

12. For more on the income and gender gaps, see Fiorina et al., *Culture War?,* 95–105 (on gender) and 134–38 (on income).

13. The Gallup numbers are from www.gallup.com/poll/1690/religion.aspx.

9 Conclusion

1. The estimate that half of America's social capital lies in religion comes from Robert D. Putnam, *Bowling Alone: The Collapse and Revival of American Community* (New York: Simon and Schuster, 2000), 66.

2. The post-9/11 uptick in attendance and its disappearance are described in Andrew Walsh, "Returning to Normalcy," *Religion in the News* 5 (Spring 2002), downloaded on 1 June 2010 from www.trincoll.edu/depts/csrpl/RINVol5No1.

Index